THE ZEN OF BEING GRUMPY

By the same author

A Guide to Climate Change Lunacy

THE ZEN OF BEING GRUMPY

MARK LAWSON

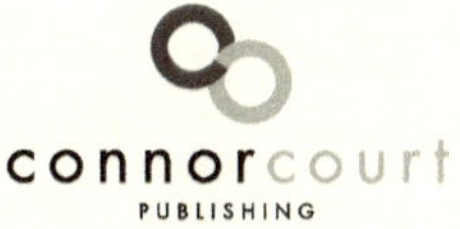

Published in 2013 by Connor Court Publishing Pty Ltd

Connor Court Publishing Pty Ltd.
PO Box 1
Ballan VIC 3342
sales@connorcourt.com
www.connorcourt.com

ISBN: 978-1-922168-34-4 (pbk.)

Cover design by Ian James

Printed in Australia

CONTENTS

Grumpy:

surly, ill-tempered

Curmudgeon: irascible,

churlish, miserly person

I

GRUMPY AND PROUD OF IT

Sitting opposite me one day while I was reading my paper on the train going to work, as I do most days, were two young people – university students to judge from their clothes and the books in their bags – enjoying one another's company. They were touching, giggling, lightly kissing and holding hands. A heart-warming picture, I hear you say? Young love? Not a bit of it. To me it was like watching those documentaries on television where they show the courting rituals and even physical act of copulation of various animals, without the advantage of being able to turn to another channel. I found their behaviour distracting, even annoying. I had to suppress the urge to snap, "for heaven's sake, stop fiddling with one another".

That irritation did not involve any moral outrage on my part. I cared not a jot about what they did to each other, with consent, out of my sight. They could be youthful and exuberant in another carriage, on top of the train, on another planet, send salacious pictures of themselves to each other on their smartphones, or whatever else young people do to each other – I am vague on that point – provided I am left to my old-fashioned, non-digital, non-iMorning chore of reading the paper as I am meant to do. I am a journalist.

Unkind people may consider this touchiness concerning romance in the morning as part of growing old and grumpy and perhaps the grumpy part is right – when the question of labelling the stages of life arises, I prefer the term advanced middle-aged – but it is a little more than that. I am not one of those angry men who wore hats whom I remember from my own younger days. They would shout at people in public if they were noisy, not Anglos (that is Greek or Italian) or were not speaking English. No, I did not snap at the couple. They were simply having fun. Instead I am claiming the right to have that urge, and not to be concerned by it. But I also reserve the right to be grumpy (Difficult? Snappy? Crabby? Take your pick) in the right situations, which would mostly involve young people who go out of their way to interact with me, or do not behave as they should when I have dealings with them. If I had been giving a seminar with those two in the front row leaping about like lambs in springtime, I might well have told them to stop fiddling, but perhaps not in an unkind way. I would have invited them to go next door where there are fewer people. They would have stopped, and the rest of the audience might have woken up enough to laugh.

So I'm not just grumpy, I am grumpy in a way that other people can live with. Here we come to the Zen part of the book's title.

Normally I have no time at all for Eastern philosophies, which I associate with people in orange robes chanting in the street, or people with beatific smiles – smiles that urge me to violence – who talk to me about karma or being at one with the universe. Right. Needless to say I have no insights into such philosophies and have no intention of acquiring any, but I am vaguely aware, having glanced at the entry in Wikipedia, that Zen is about self-realisation and the "attainment of enlightenment through experiential wisdom".

I'm hazy on what enlightenment actually means (literally it means "awakened") but as I understand it, you know you are enlightened when you attain that state, apparently after lots of meditation.

Okay from experience I realised that I am a grumpy middle-aged (in the sense that 50 is the new 40) person with mostly unpopular, often politically incorrect views and, further, I don't care. That's my piece of self-enlightenment, and it is enlightenment gained through experience – so it meets the criteria, after a fashion. Further, I reached this enlightened state without doing a moment's meditation, and without any intention of doing any. I prefer to read military history or thrillers, or play strategy computer games rather than sit and not think. But Zen, which is in Buddhism, does not quite cover all of what I want to express, so I'm going to throw in a bit of Taoism as well. Taoism is about establishing harmony with the universe, and is really big on finding flows and paths. So I have established harmony with everything else, provided that everything else minds its own business, as I am minding mine. But I will be grumpy and short-tempered with those who go out of their way to interact with me, push various pieces of what I call fluffy thinking on me, or want me to sign up to an apparently endless series of causes. Right! I have my own troubles.

I'm not saying you should not care about causes. I'm saying that you work out your own criteria for supporting, or not supporting, particular organisations, causes or charities and stick with them. For me that means entering the annual raffle for the Rural Fire Service Association – bushfires have come uncomfortably close to my house twice in 17 years – giving to a child cancer research charity which caught me in a weak moment and, for various reasons, occasionally to the Salvation Army.

Those are personal choices. In addition, I may also sponsor

a colleague or acquaintance in some charitable effort, such as to grow a moustache during November, or bicycle long distances (the trouble is they come back), but more so that they will go away or not complain about my meanness, rather than through any belief in their cause whatever it may be. So we are back to my own form of Taoism. I try to do enough to be at one with those around me, while still getting on with my own concerns.

But if your preference is not to support anything, that you believe charity fosters dependence or simply that as far as you are concerned the rest of the world should go hang as you have your own problems, that is a personal choice which should be respected. To illustrate this point, in one chapter I defend the fictional character Ebenezer Scrooge, the miser who did not want to celebrate Christmas. As we are told every Christmas, Scrooge's cause was so dire that he required drastic spiritual intervention. I ask what was so wrong with the man that required such repair work, especially considering the major injustices that occurred every day in the London of that era, with the main villains of those injustices being people who celebrated Christmas wonderfully.

In any case, the world seems to have endless troubles which cannot be solved by one person, grumpy or not.

The conversations with concerned people go something like this:

> "There is dreadful hunger in Africa."
>
> "Okay."
>
> "We'll all be wiped out by the flu, unless we wash our hands when we go to the bathroom."
>
> "Whatever."
>
> "There are more tropical diseases."

"Oh, um, I suppose I can do 5 cents per kilometre."

"But I'm growing a moustache."

"Weren't you shaving your head?"

"That was last month."

"Global warming will kill our native forests."

"Weren't they killed by acid rain in the 1980s?"

"We must preserve our environment."

"Show me a natural, running stream and I'll show you an open sewer for animal excreta."

"We must support all things green."

"Does that include scum?"

Am I ignoring looming disasters? Won't the world be a little worse off for my being indifferent to the many messages of doom? Perhaps not. In fact, I have found that crises that are ignored tend to go away of their own accord. Whatever happened to acid rain or the millennium bug? When was that swine flu scare? Has global warming gone away or is it still with us?

To look at Zen part of being grumpy from a different angle, let us return to the example of the couple on the train. I mentioned that they could be youthful on top of the train for all I cared. But what would happen if they did climb on top of the train to do whatever it is that they wanted to do? The railway authorities take a dim view of people, young or old, behaving like idiots on top of trains, so they will stop the service to get them down. That will take some time.

So if I saw them climb on top of the train, would I do something about it? I suppose I would tell the guard or the station staff. It is dangerous, and annoying and a very silly thing to do. Stop messing around and get down from there! But what would be my order of priorities? I suppose that first I would consider that my day would be put out, and then think that, well, it's a dangerous thing to do. This is another take on the Tao of being grumpy. I am not forgetting my own interests but, as it happens, those very adventurous young people will benefit from my intervention.

On another occasion coming home, I was held up for a long time because one passenger, somehow or other, managed to get himself wedged between the train and the platform, further up line. I don't believe he was injured but perhaps he had collapsed just as he was getting on or off the train. In theory I am supposed to feel sympathy for this person, but I could not see why. My thoughts, positive or negative, would not have helped or hindered this person in the slightest, and he had put my day out. In any case, it was a daft thing to do! Had I been present at this incident I might well have made some effort to free the man. After all there would not be much else to do. The train would not be going anywhere until this person had been freed.

To illustrate my attitude to the young people on top of the train and the man wedged beside it, I have used one chapter to discuss, at length, the fictional character of Darth Vader. These fictional characters are easier to use to illustrate arguments as they are much better known than most real people, living or historical. So most people would almost understand that such situations should be put to the Darth test. He would have told a storm trooper to free the wedged man and be quick about it, and sent another detail to pull the young people down from the top of the train. He would not have had them killed. If the couple on top of the train are shot by storm troopers they may fall off and obstruct the train. In the case of the wedged man there is no point. Once these human obstructions had been put to one side his staff would have dealt with them, or ignored them. Darth would have paid them no further mind at all. Darth's critics say he was a ruthless, evil man. I say he was a hard man who was just trying to hold the empire, with its system of justice, together despite the best efforts of the rebels to tear it apart to further their own ends. Darth was the ultimate grumpy person, albeit a misunderstood one, who deserves to have his reputation restored.

As for the rest of the book, perceptive readers may note a hint of criticism, here and there of young people – okay, a couple of chapters worth of abuse plus other references. There has been a marked tendency in recent decades to pretend that young people are in some way special, that they are the voice or promise, or whatever of the future. Total nonsense. Young people are just as clueless as their parents and have less experience. Why should we listen to a word they say? Why should a young person – a young entrepreneur or writer or citizen – be singled out for awards? If they are young, a decade or so of grinding in the workforce will fix that. Why should their age be a cause of celebration? Why not give awards to old people, who will stay old for much longer than young people will stay young.

Young people are especially irritating when they thrust their experiences upon you. As a last example from my twice daily train trips, I shall cite the young woman who broke up with her boyfriend, on her mobile phone, shortly before she got on the train. In the train system I use, they are now trialling quiet carriages and not a moment too soon. For the reason I know about this young person's emotional troubles is through several, loud phone conversations with her girlfriends made in front of me, again while I was trying to read the newspaper. I suppose I should have felt some sympathy for this girl, but I did not. She will recover for her emotional hurt at the same rate, with or without my good wishes, and in the meantime I have been forced to share her troubles.

A woman colleague I mentioned my encounter to remarked that it was harsh to break up over the phone. That was not the point. The point was I was put out. The tale was about me, and my annoyance at being made to listen to this tale of youthful heartbreak, not this young person.

Another strand to the Zen of grumpiness is the rejection of most of the new age and alternate therapies that seem to loom large in the public imagination these days, as well as the trend towards public activism – notably the somewhat faded interest in environmental activism. Grumpy people, whom I sometimes call curmudgeons in the book, regard activism of most kinds (there are exceptions), alternate therapies and new age what-not as being in much the same category as all other nonsense peddled by do-gooders with degrees in arts, and a government grant to do something or other. We will have none of it. Young people in particular who are into this nonsense can take their interest in the environment, along with their healing crystals, yoga mats, psychic love advice phone-in services, herbal remedies and funny types of tea and find somewhere else to play.

Am I lumping hard climate science in with the fuzziness of hippie, tree-hugging and the strange people who profess to practise witchcraft? Nope! It all has its origins in the same mind-set that civilisation is bad, consumption is sinful and the profit motive is distasteful, if not simply wrong. But instead of listening to the draining criticisms of curmudgeons like myself why don't these well meaning people show what they can do, once they set aside the destructive influences of civilisation and its greedy capitalists. There are plenty of unsewered, wind-swept areas well outside mobile phone range that would make excellent camps where they can commune with their inner selves. Or let them meditate in tents on a mountain top where they can achieve mystic peace while freezing (above 3,000 metres is good). Let them sit in circles and chant – I suppose that is what they do – and issue warnings that the world will run out of resources in just five years. This is a reasonably safe forecast because various committees will have awarded them peace prizes, and government bodies would have awarded grants, well before the five years are up and it becomes obvious to even the most determinedly gloomy that the world economy still has enough resources, thank you.

This is all fine by me, I do not even begrudge these groups some grant money if it means they stay away, and provided some fool doesn't write about them or any government is sufficiently deceived by this nonsense to let it influence public policy. Unfortunately, someone always does write hagiographic articles about all of this, and even senior public servants who should know a great deal better are taken in.

Obviously this attitude is not going to win prizes from committees comprised of people highly qualified in the arts; this approach will be derided by academics and rejected by idealistic young people who have a vague idea, having looked at the front page of a newspaper once, that the environment is under threat. But considering the quality of the pronouncements by those who do win prizes, are praised by academics and are considered role models for young people, they can keep their attitudes for those who might care. I may be unpopular and women may cross to the other side of the street when they see me coming (that used to happen before I became a curmudgeon), but not talking nonsense should confer on me a moral superiority, I hope.

Some people may read this book and consider me to be dangerously insular, preaching a message of selfishness, and that it is good to ignore the troubles of the world. Others may decide that I am liberated from the perpetual pleas of do-gooders and activists and other annoying people. I don't really care what either group thinks and that, too, is an example of the Zen of being grumpy.

II

BAH! HUMBUG!

Everyone is familiar with the story by Charles Dickens entitled *A Christmas Carol* featuring the character Ebenezer Scrooge, a miser who never celebrates Christmas, or anything at all until he is shown the error of his ways on Christmas eve by drastic spiritual intervention. In fact, as we shall see, the unreconstructed Scrooge is a good grumpy role model. His is, of course, a fictional character but one that everyone knows and so is a handy illustration of the point of the book. Scrooge had found his Zen and there were people a lot worse than he was in London at that time, so why couldn't Dickens have left him alone?

To know the unreconstructed Scrooge we can do no better than to quote Dickens at length.

> *Oh! But he was a tight-fisted hand at the grind-stone, Scrooge! A squeezing, wrenching, grasping, scraping, clutching, covetous, old sinner! Hard and sharp as flint, from which no steel had ever struck out generous fire; secret, and self-contained, and solitary as an oyster. The cold within him froze his old features, nipped his pointed nose, shrivelled his cheek, stiffened his gait; made his eyes red, his thin lips blue and spoke out shrewdly in his grating voice. A frosty rime was on his head, and on his eyebrows, and his wiry chin. He carried his own low temperature*

> *always about with him; he iced his office in the dogdays; and didn't thaw it one degree at Christmas.*
>
> *External heat and cold had little influence on Scrooge. No warmth could warm, no wintry weather chill him. No wind that blew was bitterer than he, no falling snow was more intent upon its purpose, no pelting rain less open to entreaty. Foul weather didn't know where to have him. The heaviest rain, and snow, and hail, and sleet, could boast of the advantage over him in only one respect. They often "came down" handsomely, and Scrooge never did.*
>
> *Nobody ever stopped him in the street to say, with gladsome looks, "My dear Scrooge, how are you? When will you come to see me?" No beggars implored him to bestow a trifle, no children asked him what it was o'clock, no man or woman ever once in all his life inquired the way to such and such a place, of Scrooge. Even the blind men's dogs appeared to know him; and when they saw him coming on, would tug their owners into doorways and up courts; and then would wag their tails as though they said, "No eye at all is better than an evil eye, dark master!"*
>
> *A Christmas Carol*, Charles Dickens, 1843

A powerful description indeed, and one that always warms my heart. But having set the stage, Dickens does not impute any particularly foul deeds to this prototypical miser, or perhaps prototypical grumpy person. About all that he is ever accused of, throughout the story, is that he asserts his rights. If he lent money, he expected to be repaid. If he paid a salary to his clerk he expected that clerk to work. In asserting his rights he keeps within the laws and customs of the time. He gave his clerk the day off on Christmas day without loss of wages, as that was the custom, albeit with some grumbling.

"A poor excuse for picking a man's pocket every 25th of December," he growls memorably.

Conditions at his counting house are grim with the clerk, Bob Crachitt, only allowed a tiny fire on a bitterly cold day, but then Scrooge treats himself little better. Crachitt is clearly of a different cast of mind to his employer, and would prefer better working conditions but there is no hint that he is about the leave Scrooge's firm for another counting house. Perhaps Scrooge was not such a bad employer after all?

In another scene in the story our prototypical grumpy person is asked to give to charity, and in response asks whether the prisons, or the treadmill, or the work houses, the last resort of the poor of his day, have stopped operating. When told that they were still operating he points out that they cost him money to operate, and cost enough as far as he is concerned. Although Scrooge could have given more to charity, his response has some resonance in modern times. Why should we, as individuals, make up for the failure of the government's social policies? In modern times any individual in an advanced society can point to a very large tax bill paid to support government operations, and governments can do far more to fix the many problems we see around us, with co-ordinated, properly funded programs, than any individual.

The above point is a rather tricky, ethical question which is beyond the scope of this book, although it does not advocate such a tight-fisted approach. It is very hard not to give. However, it can be said that Scrooge's response is defensible, and that leads to the question of why this attitude had to be "corrected" by powerful, spiritual intervention? What right have we to condemn someone who chooses not to give to charity, or avoids having a good time at Christmas? Was the unreconstructured Scrooge unhappy, or had he merely struck a balance with his world? Most importantly of all he had made a choice.

To add another dimension to this argument, there are people of our time who are very generous to charities but go to considerable length to avoid taxes. Their excuse is that the money just goes to pay salaries for politicians and for political rorts, an excuse that ignores the vast sums that governments pay to schools, roads, orphanages, pensions and hospitals. Do those who avoid taxes then give what they save to charities, or do they spend it buying better Christmas presents for themselves and their families? Scrooge would seem to have paid his taxes. Grumpy people by and large pay their taxes, for reasons we will discuss in a moment, it's part of the reason why they are so grumpy.

Again this is not to say that Scrooge's approach to the world around him was right, or moral. All we really need to know here is that it was his choice, and that his choice did not actively harm others. For he does not set out to attack anyone, merely insist that contracts entered into voluntarily be honoured. In that respect, Scrooge's ethical attitude is far above many of his fellow countrymen of the time. For in the 1840s England had a vast empire filled with subject peoples, and was frequently fighting with other countries – often undeveloped countries. Shortly before Dickens wrote this story, England had concluded a conflict recorded by history as the First Opium War, which was largely about forcing China to accept the opium trade. No doubt the British opium traders of the time read the Dickens story and celebrated Christmas in fine style, having profited immensely from the misery of others.

But it is Scrooge who needs to be corrected through visits from the ghost of his former partner, and then the ghosts of Christmases past, present and future. Along the way we are shown his own unhappy past. As a result of this special, spiritual attention – a major ordeal – he is converted to the joys of celebrating Christmas. Instead of being a mean-spirited employer he is kind to his clerk, and all but adopts Crachit's son Tim. The extra attention and, presumably, money spent on doctors, saves the boy from an unspecified medical condition.

That may all very nice for some people, except for grumpy people who say "Bah! Humbug!" At Christmas and mean it who will point out that celebrating Christmas in style is hardly the answer to any social problem. Tim Crachit may be better off but what about everyone else? In one of his essays, English novelist George Orwell pointed out that Dickens never seemed to have a particular policy – no overall remedy – for fixing the many social ills catalogued in his books, except that people should be kind to one another. As we have seen, people can still be kind to one another and go out of their way to make millions of Chinese miserable. Why should grumpy people be singled out as being in need of correction?

We have met a grumpy, uncharitable person supposedly so out of kilter with social norms that he requires major reform. Let us look at someone with a charitable disposition and a zest for life, this time a real person, the great American fraudster Bernie Madoff. Media reports after his arrest in 2008 stated that Madoff gave many millions to charity, including major donations to research into lymphoma and bone marrow cancer. He even had his own charitable foundation, the $19 million Madoff Family Foundation. The one flaw in this commendable generosity, and it is a big one, is that he was giving away other people's money. Madoff's investment business was discovered to be giant Ponzi scheme – a scheme where he took money on the promise of big returns, but simply used any new money that came in to pay returns to existing investors. Whatever was still in the kitty he used to pay for a lavish lifestyle, with some left over to give to charity. The scheme is supposed to have chewed up an astonishing $US65 billion, and was only discovered when Madoff ran out of new money to pay returns on the old money.

The good news is that Madoff believes in Christmas, although he is of Jewish descent. His office had a Christmas party every year of which he was reportedly the life and soul. The exception was the last one in 2009, which occurred only hours before he was arrested by the FBI. He was also very good to his staff, so it is said, and believed in holding big parties. No need for the shades of former partners to visit Madoff. The ghost of Christmas present would have been proud.

Plenty of corporate criminals in Australia knew how to party. One that comes to mind is that playboy of the West Australian corporate scene of the 1980s, Laurie Connell. Perhaps not readily remembered now, even in his stamping ground of WA, Connell's parties were legendary, all paid for by depositors in his merchant bank (a form of bank for private investors of the time). Returning to America we can point to the disaster of Penn Square Bank in Oklahoma in the early 1980s, which racked up losses somewhere north of $US500 million. The principals of that bank, by all reports, were real party guys.

Now ask yourself this, who would you prefer to have manage your money? Would you prefer cheerful bright Madoff and the senior executives at Penn Square, ever the life and soul of the party, or grumpy, miserable Scrooge who goes home to his small fire and plate of gruel on Christmas Eve? Whether Scrooge would have wanted to make a business of investing other people's money is another question, but at least Dickens does not accuse him of dishonesty.

But how can we take any general rule from that, readers may ask, as only a few examples have been cited and one of those is fictional? For every John Wayne Gacy, the American serial killer who murdered 33 people in-between stints as a volunteer clown called Pogo – another party guy – there are likely to be a hundred serial killers who are grumpy. We can further confuse things by considering the cases of American tycoons John D. Rockefeller and Andrew Carnegie, both young men around the time of the American Civil War in the 1860s. They made enormous fortunes – Rockefeller in oil and Carnegie in steel – and then gave away a good deal of their money. Carnegie had little time for religion for most of his life, but had the outlook of a Presbyterian Scot (his family moved to America when he was young). He was not a guy to get down and party. Rockefeller was a devout Baptist who thought that card playing and dancing were the diversions of the Devil (now that's grumpy for you), yet his targeted approach to philanthropy made a real difference in medicine, education and science. There have been allegations that Rockefeller gave money to divert attention from his undoubtedly sharp business practices, but a recent biography refutes this, saying that even as a poor clerk Rockefeller gave as much money as he could to charitable causes. It was in his character. That same biographer also notes that, underneath it all, the tycoon had a sly sense of humour. He is a good grumpy role model.

So refusing to dance, or play cards, or grunting at people because they try to talk to you before you've had your first cup of coffee for the day does not prevent you from being either mega-rich or a serial killer, or perhaps both. But where is the evidence that a grumpy person is any more honest than one who celebrates Christmas in style? The short answer to that is that is none, but cheerful bright people can do considerably more damage, and don't have to be very good at their jobs to get by. The cheerful, bright person may have multiple convictions for fraud and have been banned from acting as a company director for life, but he or she seems so nice that you hand your money over and walk away, convinced that it is not only safe but will earn very high returns. In fact, Madoff used a combination of charm and exclusivity. He made it hard for people to invest with him, so his services were actively sought.

A curmudgeon may also want to take his client's money and run, but he is generally unable to do so because he is not going to be trusted. As a poor dinner guest with no small talk and no interest in the sport or emphemera like celebrity gossip, curmudgeons are not going to put anyone off their guard. Grumpy people are, by definition, not the life of the party. They are not charming and bright. They cannot dazzle with witty comments and, in business, will not have a plausible answer for every question investors are likely to ask. They do not radiate confidence as they know, through experience, just how wrong they can be and are willing to admit it. This does not mean that, when they do give an answer, they are more likely to be right than confident people who sound plausible, but it does mean that the listener is likely to judge the answer on its merits. Clients will check the socially inept person's credentials and history, and perhaps even turn them away, simply because they lack charm. That means grumpy people who want to remain in business must have something to offer besides grumpiness, and that means they are usually (note I say usually) a better bet.

More importantly, a grumpy person cannot use charm to evade questions from the police, or the tax authorities. Con men may charm millions out of clients and still have time to fly to a tax haven where those millions have been transferred, despite repeated complaints from investors. In contrast, a single complaint about a few dollars missing from an account held in trust by an ill-favoured person (the grumpy person or curmudgeon) will result in the aforementioned grump being hauled into a windowless police interrogation room for a good working over. The missing money may later be found to be a miscount, but by then the charming con man is long gone and the authorities are desperate to convict someone to prove that they haven't been asleep on the job. So any tiny transgression discovered in their attack on the curmudgeon will become a hanging offence.

In other words, a grumpy person is not necessarily better informed or more intelligent or even more often right than a charmer, but they know they will be held to account for even tiny errors so they may be more careful. They certainly don't get sympathy from anyone and don't get any leeway in bending the rules – trust me.

III

JUST DON'T CALL ME DUDE

On an online opinion site I look at sometimes, predictably called onlineopinion.com.au, all sorts of articles get a run including articles urging that young people should be encouraged. One such article of a few years back urged that young people should be recognised as legitimate participants in any contemporary debate and not just as a special group to be categorised, and encouraged with token programs that achieved nothing. To effect any real change, young people should take the initiative, and that there should be special youth councils and youth advisory boards to banks. Right!

The site permits readers to post comments on the stories, and by the time I saw the piece there was a comment about what an excellent article it was, as token programs aimed at encouraging youth were rife. This was all too much for me.

I wrote:

> *Okay, I'll be the token old, grumpy one. Why do we wish to encourage young people to participate? Why can't they be left alone to decide whether they want to participate or not? After all, they have the advantage of youth, and won't want to be dragged into boring community activities unless, of course, they choose to be there. Any program*

designed to encourage youth participation will simply get those already predisposed to participate and that's it ... As for encouraging young people to go onto local councils I'm horrified. It's bad enough when their parents are on, but at least they have experience. What would young people bring to the mix?

Confused? Maybe, but it about sums up my attitude to youth involvement in anything. Young people are not in any way special; they do not possess any particular wisdom or have any particular promise. They are like older people but with less experience, much less common sense and, on the whole, are more likely that their elders and betters to go off an do odd things. This includes going overseas to work (this means they go away), falling in love (messy, distracting), breaking up with partners (boring), lining up all night to get rock concert tickets (puzzling) and backpack through Europe (exhausting).

Why do we want to encourage any of this? What part of this is supposed to indicate youth being the voice of the future? As has long been known, young people either have generally similar beliefs to those of their parents who brought them up, or gravitate towards those beliefs as they get older. In other words, young people are, on average, different from their parents only by being young. We are often lectured about the need to listen to young people because they are the voice of tomorrow. What rot! If we want to know what young people will be thinking in 20 years time, why don't we ask their parents today?

Like their parents, the youth of today are unlikely to have any special insight into the issues, beyond what they have gleaned from a glance at the front page of the newspapers as they walked past the newsagents. To update this a touch, perhaps they glanced at a news item online, while on their way to YouTube, or perhaps a friend who actually went to a news site (gasp!) has texted them. In this they are much like their parents (although their parents are more likely to have read newspapers), but without the experience to realise that they do not actually know anything much about the issue. They may tell you that they are interested in the environment – a very common answer these days – but it is unlikely that they know anything about the environment apart from what they have seen on television news or by swapping emails with friends, who also probably don't know anything, or from chatting to an activist who has all her facts wrong.

This is not to condescend to or belittle people who do not concern themselves with public affairs. There is something to be said for ignoring great events and trends in favour of your own concerns. A portion of every generation does concern themselves with public affairs, and actually makes an effort to find out about various issues. The point is that there is no reason to suppose that younger people, politically aware or not, have any advantage over their older counterparts – in fact, it's the reverse. They do not have the experience to realise that they know nothing about a particular issue. This is not to put the younger generation down, but to put them in their place as less-experienced versions of their parents, nothing more.

As for young people having any promise, individuals do, of course, just as lots of older people had promise when they were young. But others are daft, just as their parents were probably daft before them. The real problem is when they get past the youth stage and remain daft. There is lots of room manoeuvre in this, as parents may be dafter than their children, while their children will at least have a chance of becoming almost human, but first an example.

In my university days, I offered a lift to a fellow student who happened to live tolerably close to me. He knew his address but, to my astonishment, had no idea how to get back to his long-standing family home by car. He was even dismissive of the question.

"No, sorry, no idea," he said.

He lived near a railway station and the train took him to most places he wanted to go, including the university. Although his parents must have driven him places, he had never really noticed any other transportation system. This was decades before any of the green-led interest in public transport, nor was it a case of this student being above the need to know anything about roads – including the fact that his home was a short distance from a major highway, and could be reached by turning right at a major street. The existence of the street and the highway, and the fact that two intersected, had failed to made an impression on his mind. I looked up his address in a street directory. Part way home he realised he had left his library book in the student union so we ended up having to go back to get it. I regretted offering that lift. And that student was supposed to represent the future?

Another encounter I had was with a youth sent to our office for a day for work experience. Far from bursting with energy and enthusiasm for the mysterious, glamorous world of journalism (ha!), that year 10 student was unwilling to even make a pretence of any interest in the job, and wanted to slide away hours early on the pretext that he had to fill in some forms (which would have taken five minutes).

In all fairness I had another work experience student who turned out to be very good indeed and I also have no doubt that experience has long knocked sense into at least the first of my two bad examples. As for the second example, bad young workers tend to turn into bad older workers, but perhaps he found something that interested him. However, my encounters are not the sort of anecdote that is told about youths. They are never hopelessly vague and forgetful, and mostly not bad workers. They are either paragons who have the solutions to the world's problems, if only their elders will listen, or drunken, sex-mad, unemployed vandals, or pregnant. For when the media is not running stories about youth councils filled with high minded young people solving problems, they run stories about surveys of high schoolers which show that they are all constantly drunk and having sex. All I can say is that young people now seem to have a better time at school than I did. But then, I never attended any youth councils either.

Then there is the issue of awards. Whatever we may think of young people in general, if we want to think anything at all, the puzzling issue is why do we have to give them awards? If they are young, that's fine they should go off and be young. Why should they be given an award for being the young person of the year in a particular category. Why laud a novelist simply because that novelist is young. As we have noted, young people are young (as the adjective implies) but all that means is that they haven't yet had time to make themselves as miserable as their parents. Why not give the same award to a middle-aged novelist, or an old one? Why not judge books on their merits, rather than narrow the field of selection through a attribute of the author – an attribute that he or she will lose in a decade or so?

What about the Young Entrepreneur of the Year awards? There was a time when such awards were common. A business magazine, a major accountancy firm or an organisation would honour someone as the Young Entrepreneur of the Year – usually someone who was both youngish (30 or under, mostly) and who had a business which seemed to be going places. The problem with such awards was that when the business cycle turned, the young entrepreneur of the year could very easily turn into the young bankrupt of the year. Mind you, this problem is by no means confined to business awards to the young. Businessmen and women of all ages may feature on a magazine cover one month, and in bankruptcy courts the next. Those awards are no predictor of success. Perhaps for that reason they have become less common of late, or so it seems. It is too embarrassing to have the year's top youthful entrepreneur suddenly flee the country, just as his creditors close in, while the magazine issue announcing his win is still on the news stands.

An alternative would be to offer awards for old entrepreneur of the year on the grounds that the awarded person, being older and so more likely to have been in business through several cycles, is at least likely to stay solvent long enough to attend the awards night. But then we come to perhaps the saddest part of this whole awards business; who would want the title of the old entrepreneur of the year? Tactful inquiries would have to be made of potential winners, particularly if they happened to be women. A solution might be to stop qualifying the title with terms such as young or old, or perhaps award the longest-lasting entrepreneur.

Much the same observations can be made about awards for fiction (no, I don't have any of those awards, either). Writing is one area where age has some advantage. However, unlike business awards, there is no external, pitiless force such as the markets to convincingly contradict the choice of the judging panel. If the award winning book has disappointing sales it is because the reading public lacks taste, not because the judging panel was wrong, or so we are told. But if we want to laud the older generation we are faced with same problem as business awards. To be lauded as the young novelist of the year is acceptable, but who would want to be called the old novelist of the year? Perhaps it is time to stop worrying about what it says on the novelist's birth certificate, and judge books on their merits.

Putting young people down, or at least in their place, is hardly a new occupation. Daniel Defoe, one of the earliest novelists in the English Language (*Robinson Crusoe*, 1719) criticised the bad manners and disrespectful attitude of young people, and he was right. The Greek philosopher Plato (4th century BC) wanted to know what had happened to the youth of his day, and he was certainly right to disapprove – useless lot that they were.

The point is that younger people have always proved a problem, although they do grow into possibly useful older people. We should not imbue people with special powers simply because they are young.

Most years up until recently, I had some dealings with the annual crop of trainees at the place where I work. Each year I would go out of my way to give them a useful lecture which amounted to a warning that life was one long, hard struggle full of sorrow, disappointment, rejection, despair, heartache and toil, all on poor pay. I am sure that one day they will thank me for that insight, but in the years that I gave the lecture the usual reaction was to stare or mockingly thank me.

"Oh alright," I would tell them, "be optimistic if you like. Just don't call me dude!"

IV

HATING CAUSES

The bane of any grumpy person's life, and one of the reasons they are grumpy in the first place, is lectures from bright young things who insist that they know how the world works and how to put it right. This is another aspect of the youth problem mentioned in a previous chapter, in that young people not only think they know something, but often feel obliged to force their knowledge on other people. This effort to make people accept their world view may extend to arranging demonstrations. Activists, who are usually young people (a mark against them) will organise large groups of people to move through the central business district, chanting slogans about whatever. In retrospect, the late 1960s and early 1970s were the heyday of such demonstrations. The people who organised them – young at the time, but much older now – were taken seriously enough to the point of being discriminated against, and even watched by sections of the police. Governments were concerned by such events. The demonstrations could also easily turn violent, damaging people and property.

No longer. Peaceful demonstrations are seen as the right of citizens to make a point, at least in advanced countries. The police make an effort to accommodate such events, having given up surveillance of the organisers decades ago. Most sensibly of all governments also now ignore both protests and protestors, even when the protest may have support beyond the usual activist suspects. The long past invasion of Iraq comes to mind. To judge by the turnouts for those protests, a few others besides the activists believed that the invasion should not have occurred. (I have no intention of debating this point. Like most other issues used as examples in this book, readers who want to refight these battles should go online, where they will be in no-one's way). However, the government of the time took the attitude that the people who took part in such activities were not going to vote for them, no matter what they did, so why bother to make concessions? Activists hate that. They don't want to be ignored. They want to push their agenda, whatever that may be, and being persecuted is one way to draw attention to that agenda. In addition, it is all part of the romance of such activities.

The radicals of the 1960s and 1970s were long-haired, badly dressed (it was then fashionable to look scruffy), full of zeal and spouting slogans from half-understood lectures in Politics 101 and summer tutorials on Marx. This was mixed with erratic readings of their own, and inflamed by a mass media whose job it is to enrage rather than inform. In general appearance, the demonstrations of now are at least a step up from their counterparts of yore, but that is about it. Then as now these protestors have no connection with the electorate – they represent no-one except themselves – and don't know anything. Their only claim to any public voice is that they are loud and sometimes violent, although this is far less common than it was. Violence has become distinctly unfashionable in these matters.

Another major factor in this general decline in what might be described as street politics is that there are no handy "causes" about which youthful activists can rally. The Vietnam War is many decades gone, and global warming is being pushed down the public priority list by economic issues. For a time a hard-core group of demonstrators use to fly around the world to fight with police at international conferences, such as World Trade Organisation meetings. These demonstrations, which could turn violent, made for more colorful television than the staid proceedings themselves, but otherwise it was hard to take the demonstrators seriously. The problem was that the main plank of their platform, that of being against "globalisation", was somewhere between ridiculous and absurd, not to mention directly harmful to the interests of the poor people in the poor countries they affected to be defending.

A few years down the track, the same thing could be said about the Occupy Movement and, in case I am unjustly accused of political bias, the Tea Party lunatics in America. Both of those groups were born out of the same set of circumstances, namely the Global Financial Crisis, and, like the anti-globalisation movement, are entirely clueless. This is rare. Normally a protesting group has a basic, tangible grievance and is proposing some course of action, however unrealistic. The three groups mentioned above, the anti-globalisation movement, the Occupy Movement and the Tea Party group are or were all truly vacuous. They are angry but they are not sure what they are angry over or what should be done about it. For example, nothing whatever can be done about globalisation that would not do far more harm than good. But then being specific would spoil the fun, which is to get out with their friends and protest.

In any case, what makes these people so special that they can tell the rest of us what to do? Do they have better qualifications or training, or are they just angry? If they are for or against a war, globalisation, human greed, or whatever, then they should line up at the ballot box like everyone else; or run for office and see how far a protest sign gets them in influencing a suburban electorate interested mainly in jobs and (high school) education for their kids. Perhaps it is time they realised that they have one vote per person just like everyone else, so they should deal with it.

However, if they want to peacefully protest then that's fine; it is their right. The rest of us can easily ignore them. Grumpy people excel at ignoring events such as mass demonstrations. In fact they do not notice them much in the first place. This is not through any political convictions; they simply have no time for such nonsense. If the protestors want to present reasoned arguments complete with practical solutions for whatever problem has moved them to demonstrate, rather than make impassioned pleas, curmudgeons may stop ignoring them long enough to listen. Otherwise the angry, youthful demonstrators would be better off find something else to do. There have been reports that young people get drunk and have sex. Let them do that.

But protesting is just one form of raising awareness about this or that issue. Since the advent of mass media the newspapers have been filled with warnings about how the world is about to collapse thanks to various trends, and that we need to be concerned about this or that group. Curmudgeons are, in fact, kept very busy ignoring a great deal of this conscious-raising activity. Of course, on one level, curmudgeons should concern themselves over the plight of the deaf, the blind, the lame, those in minority groups, those of different sexual orientation, the poor and the mentally challenged. But sartorially challenged, body mass challenged, grumpy people of advanced middle-aged (never old, please note) have problems of their own, including being (slightly) older that the rest of the populace, the poor state of their bank accounts and the need to pay for their children's education. Problems? We can show you problems.

Then there is another set of bright young things who insist that we should at least respect, if not reach out to other cultures. This is particularly irritating as the young people spouting this nonsense seldom show any signs of attempting to understand the cultural need of their elders and betters for young people to shut up and go away. In any case we do respect other cultures and religions, to the point that we think about them just as much as those cultures think about grumpy people. If they want to hold church ceremonies that are not Anglican or Catholic that's fine, we'll stay in the bar. A street festival? We may pass through later if we have nothing better to do. No we don't want to watch a bocce game, the football is on television. As for the booths offering food from different cultures in the previously mentioned street festival, there is a perfectly good McDonald's down the road. This is not racism or discrimination but simple indifference, albeit a benign indifference – a cultural hand down from the English system. These groups can do whatever they want, provided they remain within the law. If the government decides to support them, then they should do so within reason. We have no wish to oppress them, particularly as that would mean paying attention to them.

Once we get past those do gooders, of which there are far too many, there is another set waiting to spring from the shadows. This lot will tell you that you have to think positively and eat the right foods, take spiritual journeys and be at one with nature and the environment. There is a lot of this, as a glance at a self-help section of any bookshop will demonstrate. You have to feel right about yourself, it seems, and that requires expensive spiritual healing courses. Well, guess what? As noted in the introduction we curmudgeons have arrived at self-realisation, our Zen. We are advanced middle-aged and challenged in various areas, including sartorially, and have ceased to care. We are at one with the universe to the extent that the universe and ourselves get along just fine together. If we exhibit a certain snappishness, it is because bright young things keep on telling us we have to have a positive attitude.

As for the spiritual journey, we are on a journey to the McDonald's, away from the multicultural festival, where we intend to eat whatever is most bearable on the menu. That should take care of the bit about eating the right foods – they are right for us, and talk about calories and cholesterol and the like can be saved for someone who cares. As food has a certain spiritual quality, our hypothetical journey to McDonald's also counts as a spiritual journey. We can tick that box. As for positive thoughts curmudgeons are positive that they want to be left alone, to be grumpy.

Many years ago, I interviewed a consultant who claimed that we are all on an heroic journey. I have since extended that point to the assertion that we are all heroes of our own particular saga, with its own villains and supporting cast of fellow heroes. Curmudgeons go on heroic journeys all the time, sub-quests of the main quest of life, which involve the likes of finding a McDonald's in which to have lunch. Unlike many of the heroic journeys one reads about no drama is involved. It is, after all, just a simple trip to a fast food restaurant down the road and away from the multicultural festival. But it is a satisfying goal, none the less. You get to eat and the multicultural food festival is forgotten.

The same people who burble about multicultural festivals, and there are lots of these, will talk brightly about herbal and alternative medicine, and from there it is a short slide to the real madness of psychic healing, crystals, tarot card readings, speaking with the dead and even people who seriously profess to practise witchcraft. Right! Those forms of madness may not be found at the typical multicultural festival, and there are people with a genuine interest in alternate medicine who may be offended at being linked with the likes of tarot reading and séances. But as far as curmudgeons are concerned it's all connected and, if pressed, will treat the interrupter to a short, sharp lecture on evidence-based medicine and the placebo effect, before moving on.

In the meantime, we have reached our handy McDonald's one step head of the organisers of a spiritual festival, and now want to barricade the doors. No we do not wish to buy a crystal for $1,600, or a magazine on wellness. The love life psychic advisory phone service – there are such services – will do without our business. The gentleman who wants to put us in touch with our spiritual selves can go and touch himself. As hardly needs to be said, we have no interest in the seminar on Indian spiritualism, and the book on vegan cooking will continue to gather dust on the bookstore shelves for all we care.

There is much to hate in all of this, but I will single out homeopathy, as an object of particular personal loathing. This is the belief, and it is just a belief, that some substance thought to cause the disease, or the symptoms of the disease, can be turned into a cure by being heavily diluted. The person suffering from the condition, whatever it may be, can then be cured by being fed this material. It is difficult to believe that people fall for guff like this but fall they do, and they wonder why there are curmudgeons out there who dismiss these sorts of mad beliefs in a bad-tempered, abrupt fashion.

Over the years I have considered organising a curmudgeon festival, or perhaps a festival for the socially inept. But it is difficult to think what the festival would consist of, or why the socially inept would want to make a spectacle of themselves by being in a parade. In fact both the curmudgeons and the socially inept (if they count as two, separate groups) would probably not turn up at all. After all, curmudgeons specialise in not turning up to festivals.

V

STYLE IS WASTED ON THE YOUNG

When young people are not annoying their elders and betters they are often out socialising, which is a ridiculous waste of time. Parties, social gatherings involving loud music, nightclubs, bars, pubs and cheerful restaurants are all to be avoided. They are all a good way to meet people who are boring, mentally deficient, ignorant, thoroughly opinionated, dangerous, or all those things at the same time. Far worse, they may also be young (as noted previously, this is a heavy mark against them) and unaware of your distinguished career and reputation; dismissive of it, in fact. It is also a good way to contract diseases. Sitting in a dark corner, brooding is not only less exhausting, it's safer. The Zen of being grumpy in this case, is being comfortable with your lack of socialising. If people want to waste their time in this fashion then that's fine, include us out.

If people must socially interact the ideal should be something like the night club scenes in the classic film *Casablanca*. Readers will recall (few will not have seen the film) that the participants turned up to the night club Rick's, in out-of-the-way Casablanca, in full evening dress. Even the man who had been on the run from the Nazis of the time had a classy tuxedo and bow tie and the lady, the actress Ingrid Bergman, a suitable dress. In those days, of course, even people on the run had to put up a good social front. In any case, people seemed to wear formal dress, or at least dress up to go out, far more often than they do now. Even undergraduates wore ties.

For the grumpy amongst us, the issue of what people wear to night clubs, or even university campuses, is moot, as we detest social gatherings and have no intention of going anywhere near university campuses. In those sorts of places we may encounter youths with wild-eyed, largely mistaken views on how the world works and what should be done about it. Let them be bruised and battered by reality for a few years, and read something other than the rantings of arts academics, and they may be worth conversing with. In the meantime, if we must socialise and some people seem compelled to do this, we should go back to wearing evening dress in night clubs. Men and women should wear hats out of doors, and undergraduates should wear ties and study some useful degree. (Since writing this paragraph I have seen two young people in hats of the sort my grandfather may have found familiar, so there is hope for at least that recommendation). As for youthful music and youth culture, which seem to go with this business of socialising, the first should be restrained and the second abolished by statute.

For abolishing youth culture will concentrate the minds of young people wonderfully on the point that they are not special. They are merely younger versions of older people. So they should wear ties and hats and give up the pretence of a separate culture. Admittedly this change involves very little loss to myself, as I was born middle-aged and have been growing older ever since. As a result, I never understood youth culture, even as a youth, let alone now when even the most generous of definitions I do not count as young. Need an illustration of this? Many years after they were popular I came across a reference to the Doobie Brothers. The who? No, not The Who. I understand that's another band entirely. I'm asking who were the Doobie Brothers? I have no memory of them or their songs. After trawling through Wikipedia and iTunes, I realised that I recognised at least one of their songs. If pushed, I can identify other songs and their bands. The Beatles and Elvis were too big to ignore, as was the original Abba, but otherwise I am at a loss.

My younger days were not entirely a cultural or musical blank. A part of the 1970s, the decade that style forgot, seems to have penetrated my consciousness at the time. But getting through the cultural shell of a true curmudgeon is a long, slow process. For example, I finally saw the premier youth culture film of the 1970s, *Saturday Night Fever*, more than two decades after it was released. I'm not about to start wearing a safari suit, sleeping in a circular bed, taking drugs, wearing my hair long or saying "hey man". I am still a curmudgeon after all, and we don't do that sort of thing. But I will catch up with the rest of the decade sooner or later. Those who should know better have accused me of being stuck in the 1970s. I am not stuck in the 70s just moving very slowly through it, and advocating a stylistic return to the 1940s and 50s. However, I may eventually find out who the Doobie Brothers were.

In the meantime, I am vaguely aware that youth culture is changing, even if I have little idea what it is changing from or into. I had often seen youths raise their hands with two fingers pointing up from a closed fist without realising what it meant until a chance remark at a school concert. A representation of the devil's horns? Admittedly this all developed well after the 1970s so it will be a long while before I catch up with this aspect of culture. Crowd surfing, which I also did not understand seems to have come and gone. In other words, youth culture in general I understand only in the way that an anthropologist may understand, say, the rites and practices of remote African tribes, albeit an anthropologist who has never been anywhere near Africa, hears only snippets of news about the tribes and has no real interest in the subject.

So I can see no reasons why youth culture should not be abolished as unnecessary, uninteresting and as a means of giving young people an elevated view of their station in life. Unfortunately it is never that simple. Every now and then a bright, socially-aware person (the sort who should be kept on reservations and not allowed to breed), will pop up and say that we should try to understand the culture of remote tribes, or youths or whatever. Instead of abolishing youth culture, so this line of reasoning goes, we should make an effort to study it. This is a different aspect of the problem examined in an earlier chapter, where young activists are all in favour of their peers becoming involved in public affairs, and is fundamentally flawed. Just as we don't need to involve youth in public affairs (the advanced middle-aged folk can mess things up without help, thank you), we don't need to understand them.

For the tribe of youth are making no effort to understand grumpy people, and that is the problem. Young people expect that all other age groups should make an effort to understand them, when the emphasis should be on making the young people understand everyone else. After all, they are young. Perhaps we can send them to mandatory classes in understanding advanced middle-aged persons, where they can learn about the Bee Gees (I remember them, vaguely), youth gangs of the 1950s, prostate cancer, menopause and grandparenting issues. Any foolish attempt to draw attention to the problems of youths will draw a counterblast about the problems of older people, who don't have the advantage of being young. After emerging from such classes, shaken but wiser, young people may be a little more deferential. At the very least they be wiser to the extent that they will wish they had not started this business about understanding others.

Instead of sending them all off to classes, a cheaper and perhaps more practical solution is to ignore young people entirely in the hope that they will go away. This does happen to a certain extent in that the current group of young persons grow older and so stop making claims about being special. Unfortunately they are then replaced by a fresh set of young people, who then lay claim to being the voice of the future. It's like dealing with cockroaches. Something should be done about them. Weed killer comes to mind, but the use of toxic chemicals would no doubt draw an irritating degree of comment from young people, the object of the chemical attack, about the environment. Their arguments would be aired in the media, which would be even more irritating. Have the content providers – one does not say journalists these days – nothing better to do with their time than to take sides with those best eliminated? In any case, the chemicals used may also hurt people of importance, notably those with a few years of wisdom to their credit. Weed killer is a nice idea, but it's out.

Another solution may be to go in completely the opposite direction and commission documentaries about the problems of youth, complete with interviews with the socially concerned. This will create the illusion that something is being done about youth problems, whatever they may be, and we may be spared media comment. In reality no one with a scrap of sense will bother to watch these documentaries. Middle aged people have better things to do such as watching action movies, and television series of varying oddness, or playing computer games.

An enterprising film maker may make a documentary about the problems of advanced middle-aged, grumpy people, but their efforts would attract even fewer viewers than the youth documentaries. The grumpy, middle-aged people would know perfectly well that the documentaries are just tokens. In any case, the real problem of grumpy people is having to deal with youthful idiots who think that they have some right to comment on any issue, and that point is not likely to be found in any documentary made by a concerned film maker.

Then there is the issue of fashion which is a youth thing and a particularly loathsome subject. Fashion these days seems to involve taking very young, half-starved women and dressing them up so that they look like creatures from outer space. The men's fashions are mostly a gay designer's idea of what a male would wear outdoors when, in fact, no straight guy would be caught dead in any of it. Street fashions are equally hideous. Why wear shirts outside the pants, for example? Why not wear them inside the trousers so that they do not drag around? Why do men have a perpetual two day stubble, as if they have forgotten to shave? This is mostly what younger people do, and that never made any sense. It did not make sense in Aristotle's time and still doesn't. Perhaps young people should be put somewhere else far away from their elders and betters?

In contrast, those of us in advanced middle age have long picked a style and stuck with it. Not for us the chopping and changing according to the dictates of fashion magazines, or what the latest Hollywood hero is wearing. If men wore hats in the 1950s then you will still see advanced middle-aged men wearing hats well into the 1980s (young people who wear hats don't really count in this). And why not? Constant change is confusing.

The one comfort in this is that fashions often go in circles. Thus, the men who now leave the shirts outside their pants may find that in two decades or so, younger people will be tucking their shirt tails in, and wearing hats. As we have seen the shift back to hats may be happening, and the shift will leave their elders (the present youth) satisfyingly out of fashion. This will be a return to reality and sense. But then why not short circuit the entire process, to return to the suggestion at the beginning of this chapter, and require men to wear ties and hats, and men and women to wear evening dress to night clubs. No further change will be permitted.

Those of us who are tolerably stricken in years will yearn for such fashion certainty. In that ideal world, rock bands will also be out, to be replaced by swing, and it will no longer be fashionable to be rebellious. After extensive study, albeit without having gone right through the decade, I have concluded that the 1970s was a mistake that should be reversed, and much the same could probably be said about the other decades of last century. So let us return, stylistically, to those earlier, simpler decades. With any luck the change will thoroughly confuse young people, except those already wearing hats, of course.

VI

I HATE 'I'

Young people do many thing that deserve censure but one activity that stands out, and one that many of their elders and betters don't understand, is Twittering. Although the Internet and the adoption of i-Everything has its uses, there have been excesses and one of those excesses is the craze for sending a constant stream of short messages to a group of others. The earliest form of this consisted of people sending out messages as they completed small daily events such as having coffee, or a shower. This is an abomination. Now it is commonplace to hear of radio talk show hosts, for example, having both Facebook pages and Twitter accounts. A few of my colleagues have discussed getting Twitter accounts to promote their stories and sections. Is there no end to this horror? Anyone who is truly grumpy should detest this activity as an excess on a par with whooping with delight in public, or talking on a mobile in speaker phone mode while walking on a busy street.

This craze for Twittering may have, thankfully, moved on from broadcasting the truly idiotic minutia which used to clutter cyberspace, but the practice remains so bizarre that there should be several books condemning it, not just a small part of this one. Long messages from people about what they are doing are of only marginal interest, unless there is some dramatic point to it all, let alone short ones. But even if there is some drama involved, it is difficult to see why anyone would waste a moment on this nonsense. One colleague attempted to explain Twitter-fests to me as a sort of community discussion. At 140 characters each? Those aren't discussions they are extended grunts. Why not use the discussion threads to be found on any serious forum? When an item is put on an online site, others who read it can attach comments or posts, and the permitted length runs to hundreds of words (admittedly this can be a bad thing). Either find a forum that permits posting of items at least a couple of sentences long, or find another way to waste time.

Sending multiple text messages remains bad enough, although I can almost understand the occasional text, as a convenience, as I have sent and received a handful of text messages. But sending hundreds of texts a day and Twittering does not seem to even fall into the category of creative wasting of time. Those who restage the original *Star Wars* trilogy of films using lego, condensing the films into five minutes each and putting the filmed results on YouTube, are wasting time. However, it is a waste of time I can understand and (almost) respect. The people who consumed many hours of their time with such nonsense were moving along. I hesitate to say moving forward, as I'm not sure in what direction re-enactments of films with lego points, but they were adding to something. Then there are those who participate in international air guitar competitions, Superman-lookalike and speaking like a pirate competitions (these are all genuine competitions and, no, I don't know how to enter them). These eccentric individuals are not harming anyone, and their activities are not offensive. Others who watch *Days of Our Lives* or reruns of the old cartoon series *The Jetsons* can also be said to be wasting time, but they are being entertained. It is not offensive.

Twittering, on the other hand, is so fatuous that the very thought of it is offensive. The activity is not in the category of wasting time, but of occupying time with petty drivel at 140 characters a time. It is not moving in any direction at all, except possibly down a pit and dragging the rest of humanity in there as well. Anything would be better. Why not watch reruns of the 1950s television series of *Superman* or even – and this illustrates the depths of my feelings against Twittering – reruns of *Gilligan's Island* and *Mr Ed*? It was while watching an umpteenth rerun of *Gilligan's Island* as a teenager that it dawned on me that there must be something better to do than watch television, anything at all. The people who watch reruns of those shows, as some do more than 40 years after the last episodes were made, deserve our sympathy. They are poor, twisted individuals in need of help. But I am not offended by that pastime, as I am offended by Twittering. In any case, the *Mr Ed* and *Gilligan's Island* devotees can always be reprogrammed to watch reruns of *The Jetsons*, *Lost In Space* or *F Troop*. Now that was television.

Although, as noted, the Twittering fever may have broken but it has left deep scars and practices that may never fade. Someone is to blame for this, but it is just not clear who. Legal sanctions are possible, I suppose, but not likely. The business of government has many other more pressing concerns. In any case, legal sanctions would simply drive Twittering underground, and even give it an air of romance. Those who had stopped doing it before would be drawn back to this now illegal activity. People should be educated away from this social evil, rather than prevented from doing it. Perhaps clinics can be organised and the equivalent of alcoholics anonymous set up?

Twittering is the very worst of the i-Mania, but there are other significant electronic atrocities. When mobiles first came into use,

I was horrified. People want to have phone conversations while they are walking around? Why can't those people – distressingly this included both middle-aged and young people at the time – wait until they get back to their desks, or their homes where they can sit and makes notes, if necessary. But after a time I also got a mobile as there are certain conveniences, particularly in co-ordinating families when everyone is out wandering around. If the train is delayed, or I need to be picked up from the station, I can just call.

As a result of that partial conversion I can almost understand people who have conversations on their mobile while walking around, although using the speaker attachment, so that at first glance it looks as if they are talking to themselves, is a ghastly excess. But the most difficult practice of all to understand, at least as far as mobile phones are concerned, is people who have loud conversations on them where others cannot help but listen, about what used to be described as delicate subjects. Why can't these conversations wait until they are face-to-face with the other party, or at their desks or at home and they can use a conventional phone? More importantly, why must they inflict their personal problems on others? I have no use for the problems of others, be it drunken husbands, financial crises, breakups, or children in trouble at school. Whatever. When people are having face-to-face conversations, particularly when the conversation strays into personal issues, they understand the need to keep their voices low. They also understand that they should have the conversation one remove from others, such as in a work coffee room or their own homes. For some reason, those talking on mobiles forget all those precautions and plough on.

Up to a point, and despite excesses, mobile phones are simply about communicating. However, the latest phones go far beyond the need to communicate and it is difficult to understand why.

Using these devices, I'm told enthusiastically, I can check the weather. But I can see for myself that it's raining or, if there are big, black clouds rolling over, I can deduce that it might rain later. I can access the Internet and email; but why not do that at home? I can take photographs. Right! People who do that at work get into trouble with HR, and if they do it socially they get into even bigger trouble. You may argue that they should take pictures of people only with their consent and, in particular, avoid taking pictures of young ladies who have already become wary of them.

Perhaps, but I also know of cases where people have got themselves into serious legal trouble simply by keeping salacious pictures of others, freely given, on their phones. You may argue that allowing others to find such pictures on your mobile is careless, but it is difficult to remember all the details. A more convenient approach is to ignore this feature altogether. If you want pictures take them with a camera specially designed for the purpose, for heaven's sake. Better yet, why bother with pictures at all? Why commemorate unpleasant moments? For the true curmudgeon the best moments are when they are left alone, so there is no one to take a pictures of anyway. We could take a picture of an empty room but there doesn't seem much point. If we have any control over the room we won't change anything, so it will look the same way for many years hence, which is a good thing.

Then there is the tracking function, of which I am deeply suspicious. I know where I am, and don't go to new places unless I cannot avoid it. What do I want with a device that tells me I'm in the street outside my own home? I know I'm outside my home. The new phone also lets me listen to music. Okay, I use that feature. For years I would see people jogging or walking around with earphones on, listening to music and thought that it was ridiculous. Why do they need to listen to music? Why not concentrate on where they are going? If they are on a train, why not read? Now I listen to music while I jog. It's sad, but there it is. The occasional small concession to the mania for i-Whatever, does not hurt.

Email, of which I was never suspicious, also has its uses. As far as I'm concerned that is the ultimate i-Feature and there is no need to look further. It is certainly more convenient than playing telephone tag. But I cannot understand why people need to check their email while walking around, as smart phones and tablets allow you to do. Again, why not wait until they are at a place where emails can be checked on a larger screen? Perhaps some excuse may be found for people who are on the move all day for business, but I cannot think of anything more exhausting then checking emails, and replying, while on the fly. Bear in mind that having to check emails on the run is not a sign that the person getting the emails is busy and important. Quite the contrary. There are senior executives who do not bother to look at their own email inbox at all. An assistant weeds out the fatuous and time-wasting emails, prints out whatever is left over, and puts them on the executive's desk.

The same technique can be practised with any form of communication, incidentally. Before the advent of email proper, one tax official told me that so much routine information circulated throughout the tax office – information on sexual harassment procedures, changes in policies on hiring minorities and the like – that he told his assistant to sort through it. Anything of real importance, or relevance, should be handed to him, the rest should be dumped. Email has made this tendency to generate material that is of no consequence worse, and added scam emails. But inboxes have filters and block deleting is simple, and email is too common and convenient to legislate against.

Twittering and even texting, on the other hand, increase this urge to generate trivia and time wasting messages.

While on the subject of evil, where that evil is nonsensical, I do not understand those who send and receive salacious pictures. Granted if I did it, the result would range from puzzled silence to a torrent of abuse. Legal action would be considered. People do not want salacious pictures of me in any medium, and I can't say that I blame them. But why does anyone send them? Because they can? Because it's the I equivalent of flirting? I am at a loss, but I'm not sure I want it explained. Perhaps if they send these pictures to one another, then they won't be Twittering and that is a good thing.

Then there is Facebook and LinkedIn. Much to my disgust I have a page in both social media and, again to my total disgust, I have found both sites almost useful as a way of keeping tabs on friends, former colleagues and distant relatives. I have even toyed with the idea of putting the family Christmas newsletter on my face book page. This is how much social media has taken over our lives. But having got to that level of at least using the sites, I find myself unable to engage in them. Such and such have posted new pictures. Here is a notification, and even a message! All that interaction is bad for me, I'm sure. Then there is Flickr and Instagram of which I am only dimly aware, and have no wish to find out any more about them.

It is time to put a stop to this nonsense; time to cancel the twitter accounts and use text only when necessary to do so. Our main purpose in life is not to generate nonsense, and if that means avoiding the i-Everything then so much the better. There is a whole world out there to avoid, why not go out and avoid it.

VII

MONEY CAN BUY YOU LESS GRUMPINESS

As noted in a previous chapter, of all the popular movements that have come and gone over the decades, the Occupy Movement takes first prize as the most pointless of all, although the Tea Party in the US and the now dead anti-globalisation movement would be well up in the field. As previously discussed the Occupy Movement was a reaction to the economic conditions, where the trigger for the downturn was the excesses of Wall Street, and in one sense it had a point to make in that unchecked greed triggered the Global Financial Crisis. The American financial sector had lent money to a sector of the market which, almost by definition, could not pay back its loans, and continued to lend when the housing market was showing signs of a bubble (where prices far outrun underlying market values). Other sectors of the financial services industry had packaged up these loans into what amounted to financial commodities and on-sold them, so that when the American housing bubble burst, the whole system was shocked.

But greed is a natural human condition. If conditions are right – that is, the markets are running hot – people become greedy, and that includes Wall Street dealers. The proper counter to the excesses of greed, including lending into obviously over-inflated markets is a strong regulating authority. You will note that the Tea Party and the Occupy Movement were the result of the same set of economic conditions, but the Occupy Movement does not know enough to realise that they should demand strong regulation, while the Tea Party is against such a move because it doesn't like big government. In other words they are squarely against the solution to the problem. The alternative is to not try to do anything at all about market booms and busts on the grounds that any interference in the market is a bad thing. The argument has some validity, but none of those who protested seem to realise that was a policy choice, or what it meant. Instead they seem to think there was a third choice of guaranteeing market stability by getting rid of human greed and/or governments. Right. Curmudgeons should organise an anti-lunatic protest over all of this nonsense but, sadly, no one would turn up.

As this is being written the markets have been subdued for years and show ho real sign of turning up, but when they do turn up, and even run hot, Bright Young Things appear in droves. These BYTs, both male and female, drive red Porsches and wear expensive clothes, which is a hateful thing to do, carry briefcases and insist on showing you spreadsheets on their laptops. They may also have impressive credentials, such as degrees in economics, but they are essentially peddling nonsense.

During the dot com boom around the turn of the century when share prices of anything to do with the Internet went through the roof, it was normal to value Internet companies as a multiple of their turnover. Previously, one accepted way to value a company was as a multiple of their net profits. Thus it might be acceptable for a company making a net profit of $10 million to be valued as a multiple of that profit. That multiple might be 10, depending on the industry and a host of other factors, so it would be worth $100 million. During the dot.com era, Internet companies did not have to make profits. Losses were fine. A company that turned over just $1 million, and made major losses, would be valued at $100 million, and there were very intelligent people with excellent credentials prepared to justify those crazy valuations.

This is where being grumpy helps. Grumpy people have been there before and know that young traders in well cut suits driving Porsches don't know anything and are talking total nonsense, despite their straight A university records. We know that the flash car will vanish along with their flash salary package the moment the bubble collapses. Nor do we mind if these bright young things describe us as troglodytes (literally a cave dweller) who do not understand the market. We have our Zen, whatever that might be, and we are sticking to it.

Mind you, the stock that these well-educated traders recommend at 100 times revenue on the grounds that it has "unlimited growth potential" may then go to a multiple of 200 times before the market collectively realises that all those valuations are not worth the paper they are written on, and everyone sells all at once. (All of this happened during the dot.com era, as well as before and since in countless market bubbles and collapses). The trick is to then not pay any attention to the valuations, but try to guess when that psychological break-point will be. This is impossible but curmudgeons who realise that the whole thing is nonsense to begin with are ahead of the pack. Some losses are inevitable, but hopefully will be more than offset by past profits and the joy of not returning the bright young things' desperate sales calls when the markets collapse.

As previously noted, this sort of exuberance is a world away from the present markets so no one is getting rich, or so it seems.

There are no BYTs asking you to invest your hard-earned in a lunatic stock deal, but no genuine deals either. But assuming the bright young thing or yourself had become rich, would that have made either of you happy?

There are those who would strongly disagree with the proposition that money can buy you happiness. There are many other kinds of BYTs apart from those who want to sell you dodgy investment deals. There are those who want to persuade you that money in itself does not make you happy, and they are prepared to sell you a high priced course of lectures to prove that point. They will grow rich persuading you that you are really happier without money. True riches are obtained through family life, fulfilling work and maintaining a positive attitude. Money will not buy you love, and so on. Right. Curmudgeons know that families consume money; it's what they do. Money may not buy love in the first place, but it certainly helps to maintain it. You need money to keep your family life and interpersonal relationships rolling along, and the more you have the better – up to a point.

Those who study business history often end up looking at the great American business dynasties such as the Rockefellers, the Vanderbilts and the Morgans, and the occasional odd things that can happen in such families. John D. Rockefeller, whom we have mentioned before, was so successful that he went to considerable lengths to give much of his money away, and was still left with what would be, in modern terms, many billions of dollars. This was too much money to the extent that it drew far too much attention to him and his family. Everyone sponsoring a cause, worthy and unworthy, plus a lot of con artists and dodgy businessmen sent letters or found their way to his door with all sorts of proposals. His eventual solution was to build up a large organisation, the

Rockefeller Foundation, which still exists, to both manage his money and sort out these endless proposals. His son, John D. Rockefeller Junior, was raised to have a Baptist conscience, and was schooled so thoroughly in duty and sinful ways that he was almost, but not quite, neurotic. As it was he was the most stable of the Rockerfeller descendents, with the mental health of the second generation greatly affected by the difficulties of reconciling their strict upbringing with later revelations about their father's business practices, although not all of those revelations were true or even fair.

The Vanderbilts are another case in point. The patriarch, Cornelius Vanderbilt, was a hard driving man who did not treat his children as he should have done. Despite their own upbringing his children took the trouble to raise their own offspring to be tolerably free of neuroses. That third generation eventually inherited the old man's money and enjoyed it, becoming synonymous with the late 19th early 20th century American gilded age (later generations lost much of this money and some died in poverty). However, they also inherited the family name, and it is never a good idea to be on the public radar as a rich person.

So perhaps several billion dollars and a famous name is not such a good idea. What about $10 million and anonymity? Just as rich people are described as eccentric rather than crazy, people with $10 million are not described as grumpy or cranky. Instead they are gruff and taciturn, or perhaps "a difficult study". Now we can see the trade off. You need not believe stories about billionaires who wake up one day and realise that their cook or gardener are happier than they are, perhaps because they are in better relationships. The cook and gardener are probably happy because they have long given up dreams of great wealth of their own but still ended up living in a fine house, rent free, while retaining their relationships because they did not have to work 24 hours a day to get the house. Assuming you don't want to work as a cook or a gardener, then a few million will do. If you get much more you may not be happy, but the exact trade off is up to you.

Here we come to the delicate question of our attitude to money. If you want money for its own sake then there may well be problems, particularly if you are prepared to trample on everything in your path to get it. If you want money simply to eliminate one set of cares from your life, and are prepared to stop at some point in the pursuit of it, then the money will probably make you happier than you were before (this does not mean you will be happy, but you will be happier). That is part of the Zen of Being Grumpy, knowing when to stop and smell the roses – that is, if you have the ability or the will to get some money together in the first place.

Despite the stories you see in the media every day about those who have achieved great wealth, perhaps through a hit pop song or by building up a major computer company, those people are too rare to be given much heed in the overall scheme of things. A more common way of wealth of the modest sort discussed here is to become a partner in a mid-size and up legal or accounting firm, or to start a moderately successful business which can then be sold to a larger organisation. You take your pick of these moderate success stories, you would have heard them all before. Another way, and perhaps the most common of all as its open to anyone with a relatively strong will, is to spend less than you earn, and invest the resulting savings conservatively.

This point is made and backed up by research in the book *The Millionaire Next Door* by two American academics Thomas J. Stanley and William D. Danko. In their book Stanley and Danko point out that the typical millionaire does not live in a big house and drive the latest Ferrari. Instead, he or she is much more likely to be living in a modest home and drive a second hand car. For part of the reason that they have enough money to make choices in their lives, is that they did not spend money on a large house in a top neighbourhood, or on a Ferrari. But then a lot of people like to spend money. It makes them happy. Somewhere there is there just the right trade off between spending money and saving. Part of the Zen in the Zen of Being Grumpy is finding the trade off that suits you, where ever it may be, and never mind what anyone else thinks.

But what of all those surveys you read about in the paper "proving" that really money has nothing to do with happiness? It is all about relationships, a strong sense of community, health and environment and so on. The undoubted, ongoing increase in living standards over many decades is for nothing, we are told, as we are collectively more miserable than we were before. This sort of research is usually coupled with statements about how we are really living beyond our means and that the earth has limited resources, so we should cut back on our living standards right away to stave off the inevitable collapse.

This is not the place for refuting such research or debunking the limited resources story. Those who think that community and relationships are the whole answer should ask themselves whether they would prefer to live in Zaire or Australia, Zimbabwe or Canada? If you want to live simply ask yourself whether that simple living extends to laser eye surgery for cataracts when you get older, or expert hospital care when a child becomes seriously ill? As for the bit about running out of resources, commentators of varying academic qualifications have been telling that tale since the industrial revolution. When the first oil fields were discovered and exploited in the US from 1859 (the Russian oil fields were exploited well before that), those involved were concerned that the oil could run out at any time. New fields were discovered, and then additional fields. There are those who are still concerned that really the oil will run out soon, but they are now a tiny, albeit very vocal minority. (Since writing that last sentence, the environmental movement has mostly agreed that the peak oil story is now dead). We will not waste time on the now fading global warming story except to note that it contradicts the warnings about limited resources. Emissions will stop soon, as there will not be any oil or coal to fuel industry, or so a layman untrained in social analysis might suppose.

Go ahead and consume, although it's not a good idea to be wasteful about it, and find your own Zen in spending. No one else is going to find it for you.

VIII

THE GRUMPY GUIDE TO TRAVELLING

Although it is tempting to dismiss travelling out of hand as something young people do, people of all ages get up to this nonsense, so curmudgeons must pay attention at least long enough to condemn it. For there is little point to travelling and no reason to do it, apart from the need to stop other members of the family from complaining that they are never taken anywhere. Most places are the same as the one in which you live, except that they are less convenient. But if you must travel, below are a few notes that you will never find in any tourist guide. Ignore these notes at your peril.

Going places: Travelling in any airline's cattle class is a most uncomfortable way to go anywhere. If Captain Cook had been faced with up to 24 hours in a plane to discover the South East Coast of Australia, as opposed to six months being tossed about in a ship, he might have told the Admiralty that it was not worth the trouble.

"Probably nothing down there, anyway", he would have told them.

There are supercilious people in the Northern Hemisphere who would still agree with that statement.

A full day in a train is wearing and dull, particularly as it doesn't have the airplane's in-flight entertainment system, and is noisier so it's more difficult to sleep. Travelling by car is boring and dangerous, if you get sleepy. Walking takes too long; going by horse is not much faster, tiring and there is always the danger of falling off. Bicycling requires real energy. Ships may be fine for some, but once you are on them there is not much else to do but put up with the in-ship entertainment, talk to your ghastly fellow passengers, or retreat to the bar and hope you don't get sea sick.

As for any place you might want to see, everyone else wants to see it too, particularly if the weather is warm. This means crowds and queues and further inconvenience. Famous tourist sites, the second stage of the Eiffel Tower, the Colosseum in Rome and the top of the Empire State Building – why on earth do people want to go up the top of the Empire state building? – can be so crowded as to be uncomfortable, especially in the warmer months. In all it is better, and certainly cheaper, to stay at home and play computer games. With information technology advancing in leaps and bounds you will soon be able to virtually visit famous places, both present and past, while remaining at home. This avoids queues, spending money on airplane tickets and dodgy hotels, tiresome custom and security checks, general exhaustion and crowding.

Arriving: You are tipped off the plane, jet-lagged and monstrously sick of travel only to have to negotiate an obstacle course to get your luggage. In Paris, in particular, you have to be seriously attached to your luggage to still want it after the long hike required to get to the carousels.

Places: Once you finish the uncomfortable travelling and get past the queues, you will find that famous places are smaller and much less interesting than you thought they would be. The Sphinx in Egypt is a prime example. Admittedly you don't have to queue to see it but the famous face is no bigger than a kitchen table. And you came all that way. Other places are famous for being mentioned in a song or in history, such as Piccadilly Circus in London and Union Square in San Francisco but are otherwise not worth visiting.

Information placards: These are the placards put up at spots that are thought to be of interest, which tourists are supposed to stand around and read. In some old buildings visitors could spend the entire day reading these wretched things. Why can't they simply say something to the effect that some famous person (whoever) was killed here on this date, so that the message can be comprehended at a glance; or "famous massacre occurred here centuries ago, much suffering". You can then take in the ambience – the stone work and darkness. Scary place, something bad happened here a while back, got it! Then you can move on. Some details can be added for those who don't mind standing around, feet aching while they read it. If you have any interest in the blind hatreds of a few centuries back, you can always read about it later on your tablet. They have everything on the Internet these days. Pictures are better too.

Museums: So here is a musket under glass. Musket, got it. Looks just like the pictures you've no doubt seen. Further on in the same museum you may see equipment the old explorers carted around with them; or some old Roman coins found in a set of ruins. The coins won't work on any of the modern vending machines, and the camping and wilderness shops back home have much better equipment. We should summon up the spirit of those old explorers and send them off to those shops and then ask our summoned spirits what they think of GPS units. Now that would be interesting.

Art galleries: If you see a lot of pictures one after another and they blur together. Was that set of canvasses from the French Impressionists or the Dutch masters, and are we supposed to care that there is a difference? Contemporary art is best ignored until it gets older, and then disposed of in an environmentally unsustainable way. As for statues, they provide some decoration for large, outdoor spaces and a convenient roosting place for pigeons, but serve little purpose beyond that. Why would anyone want to see a collection of them? As for antique vases, bits of ancient jewellery and delicate latticework, flea markets sell that stuff on most weekends. Admittedly the flea market stuff is not a couple of hundred years old, but it's often better made. No need to get aching feet standing around in art galleries.

Old castles: There was a big siege a few centuries back but thankfully you have missed it. Now the place is in ruins, leaving you to picture the pile of stones as it must have been in its glory days, such as they were. But it's still a pile of stones and it's time for lunch. A placard says that something really important happened there a long time ago, and a lot of people got killed. Right. Many more people got killed through disease, overwork or neglect than got themselves killed by men of high social rank who turned out to be homicidal lunatics, but then who pays attention to the little people dying of mundane causes. Whoever said that history is one damned thing after another was right. Henry Ford also once said that "history is more or less bunk" and he was right too. We are supposed to learn from history, but mostly we cannot even learn from what happened yesterday.

Rome in general: One of the few cities that has a set of ruins at its heart which it calls a tourist attraction. Why are two pillars on a slab of stone – all the remains of most of the buildings in the Roman Forum – worth preserving? Best to knock it down and put up an intact replica, complete with gift shops. Tacky? Possibly, but more interesting for tourists. If you must see anything in Rome check out the Pantheon. It's just as old as the Colosseum, give or take a century, and is intact. Otherwise the Trevi Fountain and the Spanish Steps are overrated, and the museums are too crowded.

The Sistine Chapel: If you want pictures in a church, why put them on a ceiling, especially when that ceiling is as high as that of the Sistine Chapel? Pope Julius II, who commissioned Michelangelo to paint the ceiling in the early 16th century, should have insisted on a nice flat white for the ceiling itself and asked for the paintings to be put at ground level, so that people can see them. There were already paintings there? Then put Mick's paintings somewhere else where it won't get as crowded and there would be more seats for the future billions of tourists.

Vienna: No-one seems to have told the Viennese that Mozart is several centuries dead, and that the Imperial dynasty was deposed almost a century ago, but then there are also a lot of old buildings they haven't gotten around to knocking down. Sad really.

Paris: The Eiffel Tower is one of those monuments that's famous for being famous. Originally built as the entrance way to the 1889 World's Fair, the fair has long gone but the entrance has remained. Now it doesn't do anything apart from draw tourists. If a gigantic lattice of brown iron work is your thing, then by all means go there. The snack food in the cafes nearby is tolerable. As for the rest of Paris, if gigantic stone buildings filled with paintings of 18th century scenes make you warm inside, then you may need professional help; otherwise head for Paris. An interest in statues would also help. There are plenty of buildings with statues inside, outside, up on the walls and around the door. The original builders of the cathedral, or whatever, could have built the place for a quarter of the cost if they had ditched the unnecessary frills. A few centuries later and there are a billion tourists, give or take a hundred million or so, crowding around to see these frills. Strange, but there you are.

Pisa: They should straighten that tower. Why it was not torn down soon after the mistake in the design (shallow foundations in unstable subsoil) became apparent in the late 12th century is difficult to understand. The mistake is a celebrated one, but if people like looking at mistakes there are plenty of those closer to home. Whole governments come to mind. Why travel to Italy?

San Francisco: This city's famous tram network is, is fact, quite rudimentary compared to the extensive networks in cities like Vienna and Melbourne. The one bright spot is the ruins of old Federal prison of Alcatraz. As a famous place of misery it should attract grumpy people. In its heyday in the 1950s, the prison housed the hardest, most recalcitrant of the prisoners in the US Federal system. That meant it achieved a perverse attraction for the sort of people who end up in prison. It was a badge of criminal honour to serve a few years there. Shut down by the Kennedys in the 1960s, its main use now is as a tourist site and an occasional film location. Compared to European or even Australian cities the rest of SF is of little account. The best way to get out of this city is quickly.

New York: Something can be said for the street life of this city, in that there are a lot of street vendors, but how do any of those vendors afford to live within commuting distances of where they sell tee shirts or knock-off sunglasses? All the places that you may have heard about over the years, such as Soho or Greenwich Village, have become gentrified and that means the real estate is expensive. Even in Harlem, which used to have a dreadful reputation world-wide, apartments sell for $US1 million plus. Otherwise the Statue of Liberty is an overgrown piece of terra cotta, Times Square is not much more than an intersection that may have been a town planning mistake, the Brooklyn Bridge is just a bridge and the Empire State Building is a tall building you can go to the top of, which may be a thrill for some.

Washington: Tolerable, if you like monuments, but these always look far better in films than they do in real life. They are certainly less crowded. The Lincoln Memorial, for example, looks much better in the 1950s science fiction film *The Day The Earth Stood Still*, than it does if you look at it yourself. In films, incidentally, famous places are never crowded with tourists and the main characters in them can park their late model cars very close to the monument in question. This easy access to key points in any city, including famous tourist sites, is often more difficult to believe than the ridiculous plots.

Las Vegas: This city is so tacky that it really should be a virtual model. That is, its representation should be stored on a computer. Then you can visit it without the trouble, expense and crowds. You can gamble online, why not put the whole city online? It certainly makes more sense than building replicas of the pyramids and the Eiffel tower and whatever else takes the fancy of the casino owners.

London: So you've seen Big Ben and the Tower Bridge and ridden around in the underground which, surprise, is just like undergrounds anywhere else. One difference is that there are more English people on the trains than in most other places, but that is a hazard of being in England. If you ignore them, incidentally, they don't go away. The tower holds some interest as a famous place of past misery, but the crown jewels are barely worth a glance. Westminster Abbey is tolerable if visiting tombs is your thing, which is creepy. Compared to Versailles, Buckingham Palace looks dumpy. Admitted there is a live Royal Family to live in Buck Palace but that just means that, unlike Versailles, visitor access is restricted.

Venice: If you like crumbling buildings slowly sliding under the water then by all means go to Venice. As the place lost importance in the 17th century none of the buildings have been redeveloped into something more convenient which is a shame, but there it is. Museums, old palaces, a few monuments of varying interest – yada, yada. The famous gondoliers are too expensive to be worth the trouble and if you want a trip along a canal filled with over-priced houses, a lot of new world coastal waterside developments have canals, some of which have not silted up. You can hire a rowboat for a few dollars an hour.

Amsterdam: More canals, more museums to this and that. The Dutch version of history emphasises the time when the Dutch were the masters of the sea which is hardly surprising but almost amusing if you are familiar with the British version of maritime history. There is of course the Red Light district and the looser Dutch attitude towards recreational drugs, but curmudgeons don't do those sorts of thing so it isn't relevant.

Mardi Gras of all types: These can hold some interest, I suppose, if you are not being jostled by a million other people so desperate for a thrill in their lives that they have also come to look at the spectacle, such as it is. If you can put up with displays of drunken behaviour, queues for the bathrooms and the extra chance of being assaulted and robbed for the sake of gazing at a few bizarre floats then by all means go. A better strategy is to record the telecast of the event, glance at a picture in the paper the next day, and delete the unwatched telecast two months later to make room for something more important.

Firework displays: See Mardi Gras, but the telecast does not take as long to watch so you may glance at it before deleting.

All Asian cities: Not worth visiting, unless you have business. Sure there are ancient temples and plenty of scenery in Asia, but these are mostly not in the cities which can be seriously polluted and gridlocked. Anything that is authentically Asian is modernised to be just like the West. Unless it's brand spanking new in Asia it's no good. Not fair to Asian cities? Perhaps Hong Kong is not gridlocked, but it is difficult to see why anyone would want to live there, unless they were earning a living. Perhaps the harbour is worth a look, otherwise it's the place to go when you are on your way to somewhere else.

Egypt: No Pharaoh in Egypt, in its glory days of 3,000 years or so ago, could rest in his pyramid unless he or she (there was one she) had put up another few square kilometres of statues and temples for this reason and that. If you like gigantic stone works that make no sense, unless you follow a detailed archaeological reconstruction, and endless lines of symbols that you can't be bothered learning how to read, then Egypt is the place for you. The Pyramids are just big stone buildings in the desert just outside Cairo which you can take in at a glance. There is nothing inside except for a few empty chambers which you can't visit anyway (at least you couldn't when I went there), and the local authorities don't care for you climbing on them, so all you can do is walk around them while being pestered to buy souvenirs. As for the famous Sphinx, see the entry for famous places. Cairo itself has an interesting, if seriously underfunded museum, if you can stand museums, otherwise the place should be avoided.

Beaches: If you are in an area where swimwear may be required, only to find your bathers has been left at home, you face the problem of buying some. Swimwear buying, particularly in resort towns, is not set up for the advanced middle-aged. The shops are staffed by young people with rings in their noses and stocked with bathers in primary colors with writing on them. All you can really do is choose the least eye-catching set where the words are not offensive, in the sure knowledge that you will not otherwise attract attention. Nor is there any need to go to the beach in them. If your hotel has a pool stick with that, even if the beach is a few steps away. The sand can get very hot and, when you do head into the surf, over-zealous surf life savers are always screaming at you to stay between the flags. You can find shade at the pool, without the bother of setting up a beach umbrella, order drinks and lie on a sun lounge while reading your book. If curmudgeons were given to philosophical declarations they would declare that life is a pool. Forget about beaches.

Fellow travellers: These people are in the same category as the people you meet socially, in that they may be boring, dangerous, diseased, opinionated, stupid, uninformed, unwilling to give proper credence to your own opinions (which are correct), loud, annoyingly cheerful, or all of those things at the same time. And you're stuck on a plane or a train or whatever for hours with this person. When will the agony end? Your fellow travellers may, of course, be witty, charming and pleasant but this is highly unlikely. Your companion will be 40-year-old cross dresser who is obsessed over a return to the gold standard for international trading (long story, you don't want to know).

Tour groups: Tour groups are a band of fellow travellers, as per the previous item, but unlike those in the seat next to you on a trip, you are stuck with your tour group companions for weeks. The horror! After a time the group itself splits into groups and, if there are a certain number of school teachers and social workers with the groups, it starts to feel like school. There are "cool" groups who actively sneer at the others and even, if the guide is weak or uninterested in the groups, to taunt others in the group. This is not merely idiotic but intolerable. One possibly good point to offset the main bad points is that you do see and do more in a tour group, as it is organised by professionals. If you have a high tolerance for your fellow humans then a tour group may be worthwhile. Curmudgeons should definitely stay away.

Hiking and camping: One part of the bush is much like any other part of the bush, and at the end of the day you breath in carcinogenic camp fire smoke and need a torch to see what's in your coffee. Some people like this sort of thing, I am told, but then there are individuals who like to be whipped.

IX

LEARNING TO HATE THE ENVIRONMENT

One of the great buzz words of more recent times is the environment. Bright Young Things (the BYTs mentioned with particular distain in previous chapters) seem to constantly return from overseas conferences to tell us all that sacrifices have to be made and emissions have to be saved or in five years time (usually it's five years) the world will reach a tipping point.

If curmudgeons paid any attention to this, which we don't, we might ask whether the sacrifice would extend to the BYT's salary or emissions-intensive overseas trips. Cutting out lengthy flights on large jet aircraft to environmental meetings, plus taxi rides and stays at expensive hotels, would save a lot on emissions. Not producing the many, lengthy reports that seem to be an inevitable by-product of these meetings would also save on emissions, not to mention trees. If this junket is being paid for by the government, which is often the case, then taxpayers' dollars would also be saved.

However, curmudgeons have heard it all before and know that such remarks merely result in accusations of total ignorance or of being in league with energy companies, or both. Hysterical, incoherent denunciations are possible. We also know, from hard-won experience, that there is no point in asking what happened to the report produced 10 years ago, that also set a five year deadline for action. There is even less point inquiring about declarations of almost a quarter of a century ago that the world had only 10 years to avoid climate catastrophe. Not only are reminders of past forecasts of disaster most unwelcome in this debate, the person who dares to bring up such issues is likely to be slung from the nearest lamp post by a crowd of greenies fresh from a lecture on pacifism in the environmental movement. This same frothing-at-the-mouth crowd will then be depicted as heroes in subsequent documentaries and bio-pics, which will claim that they (the greenies) were goaded to breaking point by paid agents of energy companies spreading misinformation.

Of all that nonsense, the part that really stings is the bit about being paid. Sadly, the energy companies do not seem aware of the need to pay sceptics and curmudgeons, despite many BYTs insisting that, of course, anyone who does not accept what they say as gospel truth must be in the pay of energy companies. If they are ever challenged on this point, they will triumphantly produce evidence that a few hundred thousands of dollars have been scattered here and there among various groups. Never mind the billions being spent by government departments solely concerned with climate change that now operate in developed countries everywhere – and they represent the tip of the environment funding iceberg – the comparatively small amounts given to organisations that might, conceivably, be on the other side of the debate is reprehensible. Right!

As reality is not only unwelcome but is violently rejected in this sort of debate, curmudgeons don't point any of this out, or even comment beyond a murmured "ah huh" while these things are thrust at them, particularly before the day's first cup of coffee. This is a shame as this guff often finds its way into the media, and is then, annoyingly, repeated by brash, opinionated people who think it actually means something. However, there is some evidence that the global warming-environment band wagon has moved over its peak and is now heading down the other side. The much-despised BYTs will no doubt be jumping off to find something else to lecture us all about.

Rather than reprise the now very boring debate over global warming, I will point out that curmudgeons, as a rule, do not pay attention to warnings of imminent doom and we especially do not pay attention to warnings given by BYTs. Thus we have not paid attention to warnings about acid rain killing trees (still there, and the leaves still have to be raked up), bird flu or swine flu, AIDS, the Millennium Bug, oil running out permanently and a host of others. The people who peddle this stuff seem to see the world as about to lurch into one of those Hollywood disaster movies, where resources have run out, or all but an heroic few have become zombies, or another set of heros are searching for the last piece of dry land, or fighting for the last few tins of petrol, all while becoming romantically involved.

If any of these dangers actually exist then to judge by the desperate pleadings of BYTs and scientists – who are just as fond of a good scare story as the next person – it's all too late anyway, so let the disaster come. Then the BYTs can say "I told you so" although curmudgeons would not listen to that bleating either. However, if, as is far more likely, nothing happens then the BYTs will move onto the next scare story and we still won't be listening. So there. I have noticed that once the danger is past without anything happening, no one seems to own up to apocalyptic warnings about disaster to hand. This point is particularly noticeable for the millennium bug, as that disaster – that the world's computer networks would be plunged into chaos when the date changed to 2000 – had a distinct use-by date. When the date came and went with no noticeable effect on any computer of any age, whether money had been spent on expensive consultants or not, no one owned up to issuing any warnings about the bug. With that scare and others that come to nothing, the chant is, "I never said that. When did I say that?" Other standbys are to redefine what was said, claim that the warnings resulted in the catastrophe being averted, or claim that the catastrophe did occur, we just didn't notice it much.

As no-one except difficult people (a sub set of humanity that includes curmudgeons) ever seem to remember previous warnings and forecasts, and as issuing warnings about pending holocausts is a respectable occupation, worthy of awards and acclaim, not to mention plenty of grants to study the problem, there is quite a lot of it about. In contrast, anyone who points out that the warnings are nonsense is never noticed by awards committees. As they cannot spin a good story about how something or rather must be studied in order to prevent catastrophe, then they also do not get research grants. Curmudgeons and sceptics are not only unpaid, they are unawarded. In fact, they are lucky to be invited to the awards ceremony. This is just as well, as they would not want to go to the ceremony anyway. Why watch the socially concerned with the string of nutty forecasts of impending doom to their credit, roll up to the podium to be given shining new trophies? Better to stay at home and brood.

Those who applaud such nonsense and dream up fresh awards – doomsayer of the year, perhaps – may wonder why bad tempered people avoid award ceremonies or hate the environment, which we do, with a passion. If these award-winning BYTs like the environment that is a good enough reason by itself to hate it. Whether it is a slab of scenery or a suburban garden, the environment is a potential health hazard full of germs, diseases, untreated animal excreta, and wild animals – creatures that scratch, bite or inject you with poison if, say, you happen to stand on them because you did not know they were there. Then there are tics, leeches and heaven knows what else lurking in every shrub and stand of trees, and they are all using the wilderness as a bathroom. Show me a stream flowing through a beautiful piece of bush and I'll show you an open sewer for animal excreta.

A good solution to the environmental problem is concrete but if you can't get your hands on a megatonne or two of concrete, you can at least ignore the forest/bush/outdoors/wilderness by not going anywhere near it, except at gunpoint. There are those who walk around in the outdoors and sleep in tents, or at least that is what they claim. Should this be true it is puzzling behaviour, perhaps warranting professional help, but as these people are not a danger to others then they should be left alone. One bright point is that if they walk around in the bush, the forest, the hills. or whatever, that means that they have gone away, which is good. In any case, properly appreciating the environment involves staying at six star hotels with sweeping views of the host city, which attendees at the many conferences on saving the environment have shown. Why breath in carcinogenic camp fire smoke while trying to see what is in your coffee, when you can order room service at someone else's expense, and claim that you working hard for the environment?

Cities carry their own hazards such as traffic and noisy neighbours (who may also be environmentalists), but these dangers are well understood. Nature has incalculable, exotic dangers. Environmentalists insist on warning us about global danger but overlook the danger that is, literally, lurking in our own back yards, notably the aforementioned snakes, spiders and insects of all descriptions. Concrete, however, will remove that danger, as well as cut out a lot of gardening chores. Concrete does not have to be mowed or cut back and is washed every time it rains, which can be a problem if the backyard has not been built to drain properly. But at least the rain is useful for something. If the concrete walls can be built high enough, depending on local government regulations, the noisy environmentalist neighbours can also be shut out.

Those who want green in their lives can paint the concrete a nice shade of green, and stick in a few pots with plastic plants; or perhaps artificial turf. But then why have a garden at all? Why not just have a balcony a few floors up which you can stand out on to sneer at the passers-by, who are no doubt hurrying to and from the gardening store, or environmentalist movement meetings. If people want to encourage birds, weeds, snakes and other pests in their small slice of suburban hell, that is their problem. Curmudgeons will stay indoors and put fly screens on the windows.

The other approach, diametrically opposite to the use of concrete, is to ignore your little piece of suburban hell entirely. I call this Darwinian gardening. If the plants survive then so be it. You would congratulate it on surviving your neglect, if you ever went out there. If it does not survive then perhaps whoever owns the garden after you will take it away. There may be complaints, of course, from neighbours about unsightly lawns but there is a defence to hand, particularly if those neighbours are the previously mentioned environmentalists. You can play the biodiversity card.

Every now and then environmental groups will warn that so many thousands of species are being wiped out every day. Their dire warnings stop short of actually naming any of these species, which is not surprising as only a specialist would have no trouble naming any, but then they are not talking about species that have been identified. Instead, they are talking about insects and microbes and the like with the calculations linked to loss of habitat. There are a lot of species out there. Scientists have previously estimated, through field work, how many species are in each hectare of wilderness, and they reason that the loss of every patch of wilderness means the loss of so many species of microbes and tiny insects that have yet to be identified, let alone named.

Whatever you may make of this reasoning, it is not for curmudgeons to challenge the scientists – just as we do not challenge them over global warming, rather pointing out that many deadlines have come and gone with nothing much happening. As the biodiversity warnings are temporarily convenient we will, for once, accept their reasoning. Cutting the lawn is equivalent to attacking the habitat of any number of species. We dare not do it, particularly if the environmentalist neighbours have been pestering us to do so. Where is their concern for the environment now?

X

HATING THE OFFICE

Several years ago when my boss of the time wanted to meet with me for the performance reviews which the newspaper I worked for insisted on having, the interaction was reminiscent of a dog owner trying to coax her reluctant animal into a bath.

"Come on Mark, let's go for this interview," she said, in her best, soothing voice.

"Don't wanna!"

"Come on, it won't take long. It's just me."

"Don't wanna!"

Eventually the boss coaxed me down to the street level coffee shop where I sat semi-mutinously while we went over the questions.

"What did I want to do in five years time?"

You mean, apart from have a job and hopefully more money (my employers did not want to hear the "more money" part)?

How did I rate my own performance, and how can others access your performance?

My answer was to the effect of that anyone who wanted to know about my performance should look in the newspaper. What I did was there for all to see.

There were a lot more of those questions to which I gave the briefest possible answers. My boss of the time softened this somewhat but in later reviews the brevity of my responses was noticed. Colleagues made to endure the same ritual said that I should have made up a lot of material, and praised myself to the skies, but I doubt that any of it would have made a difference. Once you get to a certain point in advanced middle age and have been with the same company for many years, your employers are not likely to fire you unless it's part of a drastic head count, in which case it doesn't matter what's in the performance review. They are also not likely to hire you. Once you get past 50, moving jobs can be tricky and never mind the performance reviews. As employers give pay rises only when they think they have to and, again no matter what it says in the reviews, those same reviews would seem to be time-wasting nonsense dreamed up by consultants and foisted on a management that wants to be seen to be doing something.

In fact, the vast bulk of management theories, a few of which are discussed in this chapter, are fair game for the truly grumpy person. Unfortunately, as curmudgeons are rarely in positions of power, nonsense such as performance reviews often has to be endured. But they do have one, small saving grace which should delight curmudgeons, in that they will make certain employers face the issue of non-performing employees who may clutter up a curmudgeon's work space.

These dud employees may be shuttled between sections, as can happen in a large organisation where the occasional passenger is inevitable and can be lost in the crowd, or they may end up as a co-worker to that difficult, grumpy person down the back, which is you. The employers will reason that a short experience of that difficult, grumpy person who does not care about the environment and who is revolted by Twittering will make anyone quit. Rather than use the local curmudgeon as a cleansing agent, the performance review process may force employers to confront their not so good worker with the unpleasant truth that they do not think that light shines out of the worker's rear end. What happens after that is an interesting question. Some employees may listen to the bad news about their performance, and make an effort to change, or leave of their own accord. A more common reaction, familiar to grumpy people but rarely to be found in management handbooks, is to blame others.

Their performance has been flawless, so the criticised employee will think, and the whole thing has been, at best, a misperception and at worst the result of a hostile management wilfully disregarding the facts. Perhaps the person in the next desk who snarls before his first cup of coffee in the morning is really to blame? Then comes the next stage of reaction, of rude lack of co-operation in even the simplest of tasks by the newly resentful employee, perhaps by claiming that the task isn't in their job description or some other previously unheard of technicality. This stage can be inconvenient for the curmudgeon (you). Management deliberately shifted this employee into the next desk in an attempt to get rid of him or her. So instead of you driving the bad worker away, the bad worker will make your working life that little bit more tedious by explaining how management is terrible (well, they may be but not for the reasons he thinks), and how if he was just left alone he could do his job perfectly. Right. The Zen of being grumpy usually does not extend to violence in the office as that can get you fired, or even shouting, as that tends to upset your co-workers.

Eventually the resentful employee's behaviour becomes so bad that management is left with no choice but to put the employee out the door, with all the subsequent legal hassle that involves.

Employees who are truly, obdurately stupid in such matters – a surprisingly common personality type – either typically learn nothing from this traumatic experience, or draw entirely the wrong conclusions. Either way, they will have acquired a whole new set of personality issues to take to their next jobs, whatever they may be. After all, concessions of error are for other people. Even if they have been boring you regularly in the office about their eastern religion which requires introspection and self-criticism, when it comes to choosing between adjusting or losing their job, they opt for rigid rejection of all change and refusal to admit any error.

In fact, refusal to admit error or failure seems to runs deep in workplace culture. I have been fired three times in my career – not retrenched, or moved on when a project has come to an end, but shown the door. One of these was from my own family's company when I was in my teens, which is a long story. I do not mind mentioning any of this as it all occurred a long time ago, but people are startled when I do. If I ever explain what I remember of the circumstances they even find excuses for me, which I find surprising. I was not making a tearful confession or looking for comfort, and I can find my own excuses thank you. A long time ago I was sacked, so what? The circumstances were not amusing at the time, but at a distance of many years they take on a comic air. I also freely admit that part of (but not all of) the fault was mine – a confession which seems to alarm people even more. In this as in many other matters, there seems to be a disconnection between myself and everyone else in the workplace (I'm sure it's everyone else's fault), so I have stopped mentioning these failures.

Although I may be honest about my past working life, I know perfectly well that I cannot be honest in a performance review. Honesty about current work events is held against you. If I should happen to point out, say, that a superior has no administrative skills or few skills of any other kind, and we have all encountered such superiors over the years, human resources (shudder!) may cast its long shadow over my desk. They will take me to a windowless room and ask detailed questions about my job satisfaction levels, and dysfunctional interpersonal work relationships. No one else is complaining about the superior, so it may just be something to do with my perception of him. Or perhaps I am the problem? Of course the reason that I am the only one saying this, is because I was the only one who was honest (that should read stupid), in the performance review. Naturally the manager concerned will get to hear of this assessment, because HR will beat him up about it, and work out where it has come from. The consequences will be dire.

That is a lot of mayhem to be caused by performance reviews, with the one saving grace being that they occasionally get a poorly performing employee out of that company, but such reviews were only primitive, early generation management consulting explosives. Long ago consultants devised the cluster-bomb version of the performance review – the 360 degree review. Instead of just bosses rating subordinates, the subordinates get to rate their bosses, and those bosses are rated by their management peers and bosses. The results handed to the bosses should, in theory, give them some idea of just how others see them. Admittedly there is some value in making truly clueless managers aware that the world's perception of them is quite different from their self-image, and like many poorly performing employees, poorly rated managers can be truly, obdurately stupid in such matters. But those managers have not got to where they are by listening to such petty drivel, and will possess enough animal cunning to strike back.

All this means that employees will normally not dare grade a bad boss as he should be graded. However, they may be partially honest if they know the boss can take a hint of criticism. These reviews are likely to rate the incompetent tyrant higher than the warm, empathetic manager who might know how to do his or her job. The good bosses are then sent off to the corporate salt mines to slave alongside the subordinates stupid enough to rate the bad bosses correctly.

Many other business techniques, designed to cause mayhem in the office and otherwise waste the time of bad-tempered people who just want to be left alone until retirement, have come and gone over the years. A few of these, some dead, some not, have been listed below. The common criterion is that they are all strange.

Knowledge management: As a phrase this mostly dead fad sounds good until you ask difficult questions such as what is knowledge and how do you manage it? Every consultant involved in this area had a different take on what it meant and, at the peak of the fad, there were a lot of consultants. But mostly it was supposed to mean finding out how the employees did what they did in their jobs and capturing this "knowledge" somehow in a system. So the knowledge was not just the selling of widgets, or decision makers that had to be contacted to sell widgets, but the salespersons' knowledge of their clients and how they talked to them, or something like that.

In reality most companies have only a vague idea what individual employees do, let alone how they do it, and getting anyone to write any of it down proved to be the most difficult part of all. Few employees have the skills to write material that is both comprehensible and useful. Getting job descriptions – that is, a half paragraph on what employees think they are supposed to be doing – is hard enough. In any case, the rate of change in business usually means that whatever was "captured" in this way would be out of date within a few years.

If a company or firm set up a system to make employees keep copies of the documents they had produced, such as leases or feasibility studies, so that someone doing similar work could find it again rather than start from scratch, that system often earned the title of knowledge management. If they were ever implemented seriously, they seemed to work. Another useful change was to keep CVs of employees in a searchable database. In both those cases for the system to work properly, management had to assign someone to ensure that the other employees took that split second to ensure the document was put in the database, and not forget about it once the KM-crazed senior executive had moved on. That is always the hard part about any innovation.

KM is notable in one other respect in that it was possible for consultants in this field, with honourable exceptions, to talk for hours on end without making any sense at all. Academics in certain fields can do this as they are not being paid to make sense, but business consultants have to touch earth every now and then or their clients, who are paying for their time, may get suspicious. KM consultants touched earth less frequently than other forms of consultants.

Re-engineering: This was a fancy way of saying let's take a look at how the business does things and get rid of the internal red tape and useless procedures that have accumulated over the years. If the organisation has been in business a while with no changes, then this may require a major upheaval. So far so good, but why give the concept a fancy name? For that matter why was the business's productivity so poor in the first place? These sorts of changes should be management stock in trade.

Workplace bullying: Yes, let's stop workplace bullying. The trouble with this idea is that the bosses are usually the bullies and rather than be lectured on how to stop themselves bullying others, they will send the people being bullied to the lectures or workshops or whatever, as a part of the bullying process. There you are, some action has been taken against the company bullies, with the added bonus that the bosses can bully the hapless employees for being behind in their work, because they had to attend the workshops on bullying.

Reverse incentives: This is not a management fad as such but generally how most companies operate. If you do a good job, the beatings stop for a time. If you do an excellent job management will give you more work. Superb work is a cause for instant dismissal, as you are showing up the managers and obviously aiming for the top job.

Total quality management: This has some value as a concept, the puzzling part is why it had to be given a separate name and made a process that had to be taught by consultants. Of course companies want to continuously improve the quality of their products and should listen to customers with complaints, or suggestions, and communicate with their employees. Why do they have to be told this, and why aren't they doing it already? But if a consultant says it, the concept sounds like a solution that can be installed, like a piece of software. The board may put off a planned drastic management reorganisation if they are told that the company will install TQM, whatever it may be. Quality management systems cannot be installed, of course, and the company should already be doing it as part of the business, but the phrase sounds good and that's all that matters.

Management consultants: The previous point dealt with a

particular case of a company management grasping for any solution that sounded good to the board, in order to deflect the board from its planned management reorganisation, including a change in chief executive. Management consultants can be very good and even of some use, but they also can be and often are enlisted in the cause of saving the management director's job by being seen to be doing something. Why management consultants would know more about the industry and the company than the executives who have been working in the area for years is difficult to understand. But the consultants do know more about concepts such as TQM and can install that, whatever it may be. When the managing director runs out of plausible excuses, has already hired three sets of management consultants to no avail, and cannot convincingly shift the blame, the world will be told that he or she has decided to spend more time with their families. The newcomer will then have to start the process of fooling the board all over again.

Management books: Curmudgeons, by their nature, do not make understanding empathetic managers. Employees should do their work or find some other place, and payroll, to mess around on. Provided the work is done and the curmudgeon manager is left in peace, then he or she is unlikely to fire anyone or trouble themselves over minor matters in the office. They do not make inspiring leaders, but they also do not get in the way, so they are several steps ahead of those who apply the latest theories from books on management. These can make interesting reading, and the ones that rely on historical analysis can be informative but are they useful when it comes to actually managing anything? I think not.

The idea is to analyse the problem and they try to apply a solution, preferably not a cardboard cut-out solution from a management book, but an actual solution that suits the circumstances. If the solution does not work, the manager should go back to the drawing board and try something else. That is the ideal approach. The more common approach, once the initial solution has been tried and failed, is for the leader to insist that he (males are far more likely to be silly in this respect) had been right all along, and really it was the employees who let him down. The solution is than to fire the employees who did their best to make the manager's idea work and get in a new lot but, above all, continue with the solution that does not work. As we saw earlier errors can never be admitted, and it's always the other person's fault.

XI

THE GRUMPY BUT GOOD GUY WHO LOST

One of the ultimate grumpy people, a curmudgeon-and-a-half if there ever was one, is the fictional character Darth Vader. But despite the fact that he is fictional we can learn a lot from our good friend Darth. For a little knowledge of real history indicates that the man may not be so bad after all and, in fact, the real villains of the piece are the fun-loving adventurous heroes of the films. If he had not lost the war, Darth might have been an excellent grumpy role model. As it is, an investigation of his life and work serves as a reminder to the truly grumpy of us all, that grumpiness is not all bad, albeit seldom well rewarded.

Everyone is familiar with the six *Star Wars* films covering the half century or so in which the Galactic Republic became an Empire, and the eventual success of a rebellion against that Empire. At the end of the series the Emperor dies, as does his chief Lieutenant Darth Vader. Besides the films there are a number of books detailing the supposed historical background of the stories complete with talk of trade federations and elected queens and the like. My contention is that all of this material is little more than detailed legends. If we use knowledge of earth history as a tool to scrape away these accretions of legend a more complicated and far more morally ambiguous tale emerges – one in which the heroes lose much of their sheen and the villains brush up well. Neither the Emperor nor Darth Vader were innocent by any means, and the "good guys" retain some good, but the picture is a more balanced one.

Films or plays supposedly about historical events rarely have much connection with those events, and may be almost entirely at odds with the known history. The chief exhibit in the case against the performing arts as a useful guide to history, any history, is the Shakespearian play *Richard III.* The play is one of the greatest dramas in the English language of course but, as has long been recognised, has very little connection with the historical English King.

In fact, Richard III serves as a good historical model for Darth Vader in one respect. He is always portrayed as a misshapen hunchback when in real life he had no particular deformities. Similarly with Darth Vader, we can guess that the black suit, black full-face helmet and heavy breathing were probably added to the story by later writers, to make the character more menacing. Just as various black deeds have been attributed to Darth, writers under the control of the winning side have declared Richard guilty of various crimes, including ordering the deaths of his nephews, Princes Edward and Richard. Historians can agree that Richard III was an able administrator and certainly not notably cruel or ruthless – at least as far as Royal personalities in those times went – but have been unable to decide whether he did order his nephews to be murdered. Of two recently published books on the issue at the time of writing, one says maybe yes and the other says maybe no. My money, for what it is worth, is on the Duke of Buckingham – everyone was ambitious for the crown back then – but the matter is unlikely to ever be resolved.

Just as Richard's reputation suffered because later fiction was written by playwrights who preferred to stay out of Tudor prisons, those who wrote down the original *Star Wars* tales would have been keen to avoid the New Republic's infamous interrogation centre (motto: The truth shall set your spirit free). After all, the unlikely triumvirate of Princess Leia, Luke Skywalker and Hans Solo had already shown they would stop at nothing to gain power. Of Darth Vader's many supposed dark deeds only two – bar a couple of minor massacres as a young man – are really spelt out. These are the destruction of the Jedi order of which he was a member, including the slaughter of very young recruits, and being complicit in the destruction of the planet Alderaan as a demonstration of the power of the Empire's Death Star. All this would seem to be very heavily slanted against Darth and show Leia, Solo and Skywalker in a blinding white light. Right!

On the accusation concerning the Jedi order Vader has a case to answer, but he may also have a defence. For elite groups such as the Jedis have always proved a problem. Examples that come to mind include the Varangian Guard (Byzantine Empire), the Praetorian Guard (Roman Empire), the Janissaries (Ottoman), and the Moscow Streltsy. Other organisations that may have some parallel to the Jedis are the orders of knight-monks of the middle ages, such as the Hospitallers and the Knights Templar.

The first three episodes (the last three to be filmed), and various attendant literature, indicate that the Jedi Knights were a sort-of para-military police force whose members went around putting down potential threats to the order of the Empire, as well as occasionally acting as glorified bodyguards. The Jedis took requests from the original Republic in setting missions for their members, but there was no established chain of political command of the order, or seemingly any form of external supervision. Instead, the order considered itself the independent arbiters of justice in the galaxy, and meddled in politics.

We will pass over various points of interest in the Jedis' role, such as the order's apparent lack of a prison system or lawyers, despite its police function, and on to our analogy with the various military guards mentioned above. All of those elites were founded with the best of intentions and filled mixed roles in their respective empires. The Praetorians and the Streltsy acted as police at different times, but they were palace guards and eventually meddled in politics in some way. They would murder one Emperor and proclaim another. The Ottoman Janissaries, in particular, became a powerful political bloc, and are perhaps the best analogy in earth history to the Jedi.

In their prime – the 15th and 16th centuries – the Janissaries were the fighting elite of the Ottoman Empire. Made up of Christian boys taken from their families very young and forcibly converted to Islam, they were initially not permitted any other life or to marry. (Do you see some similarities with Jedis here?) By the early 18th century, however, Janissaries had families – membership had become hereditary – and they had become a powerful part of the government, able to dictate policy and change Sultans as they wished through Palace coups. To make matters worse they had lost their military effectiveness – the musket, bayonets and cannon of the European armies were much better – but they resisted all attempts at modernising the military, as any change meant a possible loss of privileges. Eventually the sultan Mahmoud II decided to get rid of the Janissaries once and for all and, when they revolted yet again in 1826, had most of them killed in a major street battle. The rest were executed or banished.

There we have the most likely scenario. The Jedi were an elite palace guard that also at times acted as a police force, but which had long ceased to be of any military use. The films play up the effectiveness of "the force" with its good side and bad side, but most of the feats performed by the characters in those films can be dismissed out of hand. Anyone trained in martial arts who has sat through any of the Hollywood or Asian films in which martial arts feature will know that these things get exaggerated. In any case, if one is feeling aggressive then a sub-machine gun is difficult to beat at close quarters. The films show Jedi using their light sabres to deflect bullets (or the equivalent of bullets) from robot soldiers but that is scarcely credible. Go with the guy with the Uzi.

Despite the order's posturing the Jedi were tolerated as a cheap form of military until a real war broke out with the Sith-bloc. The films portray the Sith as an order rivalling that of the Jedis but using the dark side of the human character, as opposed to the light or good side used by the Jedis. Let's all have a good laugh at that, and get it out of the way. Episode I (the fourth film to be made) also talks of a Trade Federation – who are mostly non-human – but Episode III mentions separatists. In the opening scenes of that film we are told a separatist fleet has managed to get all the way to Coruscant, the capital of the Galactic Republic (as it then was) to kidnap the Republic's head of government, Supreme Chancellor Palpatine.

Another, much more likely take on all of this is that the Sith-Trade Federation-Separatists are all one and the same thing with perhaps a few Republic systems siding with the Sith-bloc, especially when they were likely to be overrun. Palpatine's kidnapping was explained away as some sort of deep plot, as he was to turn into the evil emperor, but the fact remains that an invading fleet had penetrated as far as the seat of government. The war had the Galactic Republic seriously unprepared, and Palpatine had to reform the military quickly. Unfortunately, the Jedis were in the way.

The Jedis still thought in terms of heroic hand-to-hand combat, of closing until one could see the whites of the enemies' eyes, and then duelling with light sabres! But technology had long moved on to clone armies – hence the name of the wars – controlled by a few, highly skilled personnel who rarely strayed from control consoles. The Jedis would have considered remote control beneath them and, in any case, thought of themselves as the sole guardian of the "right way" or "the force" as they put it. That meant no one could tell them how to fight.

More importantly, reform meant that they would lose their privileges and powers, including the order's vast wealth. At no point in any of the films are we told where the order got the money to operate its extensive facilities, but perhaps it was like the Hospitallers and the Knights Templar in that it relied on donations – notably contributions from deceased estates. Wealthy business persons who wanted to ensure that their soon to depart spirit would be looked after by the force, would remember the Jedis in their wills. The Templars used to act as international bankers, and had a sizable non-military arm administering its holdings, so perhaps the Jedis ran a major galactic bank (motto: Defaulters will feel the force).

Then there was the question of the private security operations run by individual Jedis, which unsympathetic Imperial officials permitted to investigate them might describe as protection rackets. No, as far as the Jedis were concerned, reform was out of the question, and they could get to any Republic politician who thought otherwise. However, with the Republic's outer defences being overrun and even its core under attack a desperate Senate caved in to a demand by Palpatine, undoubtedly an opportunistic politician, for dictatorial powers. Palpatine then turned to a Republic general,

Darth Vader, to eliminate the Jedis, as a necessary first step towards restoring military sanity. A bonus was that the order's wealth could be confiscated by the Republic and certain loans to highly placed Republic officials could be wiped off the Jedi banking books. In this the fate of the Jedis parallels that of the order of the Templars, which was dissolved by the Philip IV of France in the 14th century largely because Philip IV owed a huge sum to the order. He had borrowed to finance war with the English, and preferred not to repay.

As Darth is a Sith title, Darth Vader was probably a renegade Sith, whatever they may be. To judge from the later actions of the adventurer Luke Skywalker, and as the films also indicate, Vader could also claim membership of the Jedi order. Just how that came about need not detain us here. He was certainly the man for the job, but despite his undoubted ruthlessness he did not kill gratuitously. Once Senator Palpatine had ordered the Jedi to be disbanded, no doubt in a surprise declaration, Darth would have shut off all services to the Jedi facilities, stopped its trading facilities (highly inconvenient to the markets at the time) and frozen all assets. Then he would have offered the Jedis a choice of exile or elimination. A number accepted military posts on the Federation's frontier. However, a handful of diehards chose to lock themselves up in the citadel and fight to the last person. As the order's members were always trained from a very young age and by then membership had become hereditary, there would have been children in the citadel and a number may have been killed in the final shoot out. That was unfortunate, but the situation was desperate.

Having dealt with a major internal problem, the Republic, now tightly controlled by Palpatine, was free to fight the external foe but with very little time to modernise. Some Republic systems may have co-operated, but the fight seems to have been mainly Sith-bloc or trade federation versus The Republic. As subsequent films indicate the Republic took a couple of big hits, including the loss of key star systems. But the Vader-led forces made enough of a comeback for Palpatine to patch together a shaky peace – one that recognised Sith-bloc gains but gave the Republic a breathing space in which to build up and modernise its seriously antiquated forces.

Although necessary that truce would have horrified a majority of senators. They had not put Palpatine in charge, just to make a truce with key systems still in Sith-bloc hands. Why had he not performed a miracle at no extra cost? In any case, if the immediate crisis was over they thought that Palpatine should hand back his dictatorial powers. Then there was the vexed question of the additional taxation required to pay for the modernisation of the armed forces. The Jedis had been substantially self-financing. Power blocs led by ambitious senators who thought they could do just as good a job as Palpatine, began to emerge. With the Senate no longer functioning as a governing body, Palpatine declared himself Emperor, and disbanded it. He was not reluctant to do so – he liked the idea of being Emperor – but he did have reasons for making the declaration.

All was quiet for some years but then a major group of planets on the other side of the Federation to the Sith-bloc and one of the aforementioned quarrelling factions declared themselves independent, in part over the quite separate issue of Droid rights, but also because they did not want to pay the Imperial taxes which had been increased to fund modern defence forces.

The Rebels that Darth Vader had to put down were, in essence, economic rebels. They resented the taxation required to pay for the modernisation of the Imperial military, just as the American colonists resented being made to pay for their own defence, and on top of that they were about to lose the Droids as a compliant work force. As fans of the *Star Wars* series will recall, in the fourth episode (the first to be produced) the two Droids R2-D2 and C3PO try to follow Obi-wan Kenobi and Luke Skywalker into a low bar on a planet called Tatooie, only to be ordered out by the barman. "No Droids in here." Droids were the lowest of the low, not even permitted to be seen socialising with space scum. Imagine the reaction of the planets who had relied on Droids to do the work (so that the humans and other species could hang around in bars), when the Empire announced that it planned to recognise Droids as Imperial citizens.

The rest of the empire had moved onto collective artificial intelligences controlling robot units which did the work. The systems that rebelled still preferred the approach of using Droid units with separate personalities, which had some advantages in flexibility and access for ordinary citizens. The use of Droids better suited the lower density populations of the rebel planets, and could be bought and sold more easily that the giant AI units of the Imperial core. In hindsight, this move was an unfortunate one on the part of the Emperor, but most likely he was trying to placate powerful AI-run planets that had arisen and completely under-estimated the strength of the reaction from fringe states. The Senate might have at least made him aware of this folly, but it had been disbanded.

So when various systems were asked to pay higher taxes and undertake a major economic reorganisation, all at the behest of a remote administration that had lost a war, they rebelled. As part of declaring their independence the Rebels took the extraordinary step of forming their own Jedi Knights with a leading member, Luke Skywalker, taking the equally extraordinary step of declaring himself to be Darth Vader's son!

Skywalker's claim to be a misplaced son of Darth Vader is difficult to believe, despite the dramatic revelation in the fifth episode (the second to be produced). The same can be said for equally bizarre claim that Princess Leila (a nick name rather than an actual title) is a misplaced daughter of the same General. Children cannot be misplaced so frequently and easily in an advanced society with electronic tracking and DNA tests and, in any case, the claims are too convenient.

As we have seen, true Jedi Knights, with rare exceptions, had to be born into the order and Vader was technically the only remaining Jedi. When he eliminated the Jedis he took the title of Grand Master for himself, probably because the office of Grand Master had some relevance under the old constitution, and never dropped it. A supposed son of the Grand Master could then become a Jedi, somewhat late in life, with a pretence of legitimacy. Skywalker's claim to be the son of Vader hidden from him because the General had "turned to the dark side", may even have been faintly plausible to contemporaries. Vader probably could not remember exactly which women he had been with at what times, and the sexual exploits of Skywalker's mother, Princess Padmé Amidala, were notorious. Note that the marriage that allegedly took place between Vader and Princess Amidala, a women several years his senior, had to be kept secret due to the Jedi rules – so secret that no record of it or witness to it was ever found. It is not clear why Princess Leila also chose to claim to be a daughter of Vader. Perhaps it was already known that she and Skywalker were siblings or perhaps, to give the propaganda campaign against the Imperium that extra edge, it was decided to set up a high-profile Jedi Knights Women's section.

The Rebel Alliance was not about to readopt the Jedi approach to military matters, but once re-established, the order became a convenient stick with which to beat the Imperium in general and Vader in particular. "We are now the keepers of the right way [or the force, or whatever] and have re-established the order so brutally wiped out by Vader, who then lost the war. That's what we are fighting about." The backup arguments involved long, heart-felt diatribes about heavy Imperial taxation. The issue of Droids' rights was dealt with, if it was mentioned at all, in vague statements about consultation.

While this propaganda battle went on, both sides prepared for the inevitable military showdown. Realising that something had to be done about a suddenly troublesome backwater, or he would lose more systems, the Emperor dispatched Vader with whatever Imperial forces could be spared from watching the Sith-bloc. The rebel systems hurriedly assembled any military forces they could find. As can be seen from the films, the rebels were not ragged and hungry Maoist rebels emerging from jungle bases to ambush army patrols. They were well organised, well financed and equipped with weapon systems capable of taking the battle to the Imperial forces. But crucially they did not have the money or time to produce Death Stars – moon-sized stations capable of blowing up entire planets. Instead they were forced to find ways to counter them with weapons they could produce in perhaps five years or less. In this they were fortunate in that the Imperial reliance on Death Stars as the mainstay of their battle fleets ultimately proved disastrous – although not quite in the way depicted in the films.

Here we come to the issue of the stolen plans of the Death Star which the so-called Princess Leia was trying to get to the Rebel Alliance at the beginning of the original *Star Wars* film. Note that she was engaged in espionage while on a supposedly diplomatic mission (in the film she tries to claim diplomatic immunity). Vader had every right to use reasonable force to detain a diplomat if that diplomat happened to be actively spying, and use whatever force seemed appropriate to regain possession of vital military information. But he would have had to hand Leia back to her own Government, which was probably how she managed to "escape", and never mind the unlikely series of adventures in the film. Before she was handed back, however, Vader allegedly made her witness the destruction of the heavily-populated planet Alderaan.

This allegation is difficult to believe. In the film the order to destroy the planet is not given by Vader, but by a Governor Tarkin (played by English actor Peter Cushing in fine form). Vader made Princess Leia watch. But no Imperial servant, no matter what their degree of sanity, would wipe out a planet full of taxpayers without a very good reason. A much more likely explanation is that Alderaan was thinly inhabited, perhaps a barren chuck of rock with mining operations and a rebel alliance military base which the Death Star destroyed in a blink. The alliance then realised, with a shock, that it had a problem. Its own attack planes had to be launched from something, and that base could be destroyed the moment the Death Star got within range – say, half a solar system or so away. But the Empire was unlikely to have had more than one Death Star, and had to be careful with it.

If the gigantic craft was seriously damaged it would have to be sent all the way back to an Imperial naval shipyard, and might not return for years. The sixth episode suggests that an entirely new Death Star was built above a heavily forested moon inhabited only by cute, teddy bear-like natives. No. When something as complex as a Death Star requires extensive repairs, serious industrial capacity, specialised machinery and considerable expertise are required to fix it.

We can also dismiss, out of hand, the apparent propensity of these Death Stars to blow up, as if they are early 20th century battleships keeping large magazines filled with cordite. Nuclear reactors melt down if interfered with, or explode conventionally and spew radioactive material everywhere as one did at Chernobyl. Most of the battle scenes in the films are similarly ridiculous. The small space fighter craft behave exactly as if they are aeroplanes in an atmosphere; no-one thinks twice about firing blasters in a spaceship; even supposedly trained personnel stick their head above cover to see if the enemy that just shot at them is still there, and so on. The armoured Walkers shown in the fifth and sixth instalments, incidentally, would be of no conceivable use on a 21st century earth battlefield, where armoured vehicles only show themselves to shoot, let alone on a battlefield of the future. It is possible that the Walkers were antiquated left-overs from the Jedi era, only intended for crowd control – hence the slow movement and lack of armament All the modern stuff was required to keep the Sith-bloc in check, and rebel front got the left overs, apart from the Death Star.

So here is the likely sequence of events for the fourth, fifth and sixth episodes. The Rebels managed to steal a set of plans for the Death Star which helped them to damage the craft, but at great cost to their fleet. Vader decided not to send the damaged Death Star back to an Imperial shipyard. Instead he parked it above one of the industrialised rebel worlds, and sent for skilled personnel. As the world was probably forced to pay for the repairs, in addition to Imperial taxation, there would have been considerable bitterness. This was probably the true origin of Vader's later very bad reputation.

In the meantime, the remnants of the rebel forces were chased around different systems, with their leaders dreading the time a repaired Death Star entered the fray. Now we come to the climax of the six films, and the destruction of the Death Star supposedly in construction. As noted there was only one Death Star. It was damaged in the first battle then parked above an industrialised planet for repairs – a planet resentful over being made to pay for those repairs, with that resentment being stoked by Rebel Alliance agents, including the shadowy, sinister Hans Solo.

The image of Hans Solo presented in the films is that of a knock-about, small-time smuggler with a single, poorly-maintained ship. Rebellions are not made by such persons. Instead, he was probably a gangster operating on the fringes of the Imperium, who saw his chance in the Rebellion and made contact with the farm boy-turned-Rebel Alliance strong man, Luke Skywalker. The films make Skywalker out to be a likable, guileless farm boy who eventually realises his destiny to become a serious-minded Jedi. Although Skywalker preferred to be known as a Jedi he was obviously a key figure in the Alliance, as was his supposed sister Princess Leia. As troubled times tend to bring forth ruthless leaders, it would not have been safe to cross either of them. Whatever he was like in real life, Skywalker gave some assistance to Solo, including help in eliminating rival gangster Jabba the Hut, in return for various services such as transportation at crucial times, and help in sabotaging the repairing Death Star.

Very likely Solo financed the operation and helped suborn Imperial personnel. Luring officials into compromising situations and then blackmailing them is an ancient art. Once blackmail had opened a window of opportunity the assault teams led by Skywalker would have struck hard and fast. Vader went down with his ship, which is a shame as he was trying to do his job in holding the Empire together, and for the sake of a worthy cause – Droid empowerment. Some of his measures would now be considered harsh but those were difficult times.

That final disaster and loss of his best general proved too much for the sanity of the Emperor, already at his wit's end over the problems caused by the Clone wars, and he became an impotent figure, wandering from room to room in his huge palace muttering to himself. The Empire quickly broke up into quarrelling fragments, several of which were annexed by the Sith. Skywalker, Hans Solo and Leia managed to grab considerable power for themselves in the newly independent systems, which happened to be well away from the Sith bloc areas, and made sure that the histories gave their version of events.

That meant that poor Darth Vader has never been allowed to set the record straight. He was undoubtedly a hard man and certainly a curmudgeon but he did not deserve the bad press he received. But then it is always the fate of grumpy people who lose to be thoroughly vilified. History is written to favour the villains who win.

XII

THE CURMUDGEON PHRASE BOOK

Awesome – nothing is ever awesome, so there is no need to use the word. Some things are tolerated, or acknowledged with a grunt and other things are either ignored or snarled at, depending on the exact state of your temper. But they are never awesome.

Bah! Humbug!: Good words that should be used often, particularly at Christmas.

Bright Young Things: People who are young, as far as you can remember what young people look like, who insist on telling you how the world works and what we should do about it, and all before your first cup of coffee in the morning. They may also bounce around at the same time. They should be subject to control orders and put on reservations, but sadly they are not.

Christmas: Idiotic festival when they put fake decorated trees in the middle of shopping centres and hang tinsel from the ceilings. Some fools are sure to sing carols; others will say "Ho, ho, ho!" Presents? It's easier to buy your own. People should find something better to do with their time.

Dude: Young people use this word to one another, so advanced middle-aged grumpy people do not.

Empowerment: A lot of people want to be empowered, but are we stopping them? Rather than have someone make idiotic decisions for them, they want to make their own idiotic decisions. No-one can object to this provided they go somewhere, far away, to make them.

Environment: Something to be avoided by hiding in cities, large aircraft and hotel rooms. Good heating and air conditioning is recommended. The environment is full of exotic, poisonous, dangerous creatures all of which use the outdoors as their bathroom. No wonder the place is so polluted. If you want to look at trees and the like, and it takes all kinds, then there is excellent material on the Internet.

Hateful: Almost everything is.

Inclusiveness: Curmudgeons do not want to be included in decision-making, particularly when it involves community matters and the decision-making is being led by Bright Young Things. Other groups can be included, as far as they care, provided the process is not inflicted on them.

Like: Curmudgeons are, like, over the use of that word.

Parties: Like all social gatherings these are for young people who go to them, one assumes, to meet other young people, although it is difficult to understand why they would want to. There may also be drinking and perhaps loud music. One end result in some cases, I am told, is the sex act, but it is to be hoped that this occurs indoors. To have it occur out in the street is too distracting.

Raising awareness: So why don't the people who use this phrase become aware of the plight of curmudgeons who have to put up with people who use that phrase, and go away.

www.ingramcontent.com/pod-product-compliance
Lightning Source LLC
LaVergne TN
LVHW091010080826
845145LV00003B/1209

* 9 7 8 1 9 2 2 1 6 8 3 4 4 *